EMILY EXPLAINS THE SWISS

This book is dedicated to my grade 8 teacher Mrs. Willis, who—after reading one of my short stories—asked me to dedicate my first book to her. For all I know, she asked this of every 13 year old who passed through her classroom to hedge her bets, but I can't ask her now, because she's dead. RIP Mrs. Willis.

EMILY EXPLAINS THE SWISS

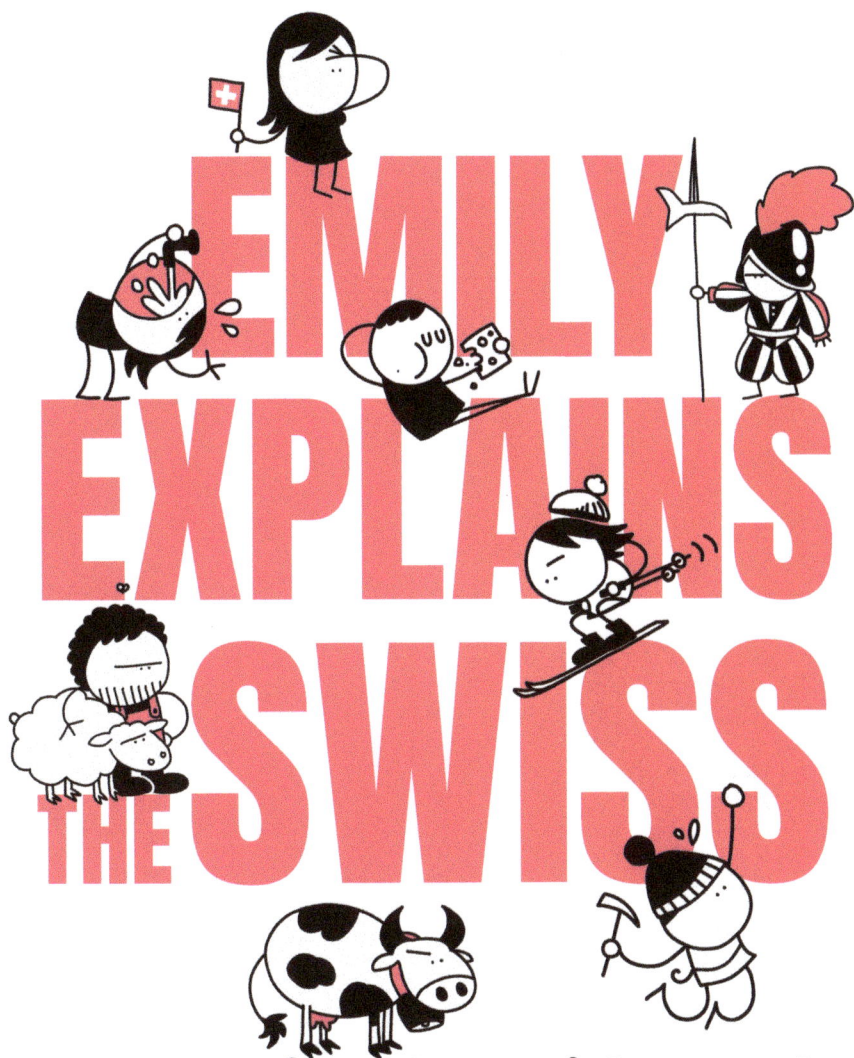

An Outsider's Inside Look from Apéro to Zurich

Author
Emily Engkent

Illustrator
PanpanCucul

Emily Explains the Swiss
An Outsider's Inside Look From Apéro to Zurich
ISBN: 978-3-03869-154-9

© 2023, Bergli Books, an imprint of HELVETIQ (Helvetiq SA),
Mittlere Strasse 4, CH-4056 Basel, all rights reserved.

Text © Emily Engkent, all rights reserved.
Illustrations: PanpanCucul
Layout and typesetting: Elżbieta Kownacka
Editor: Richard Harvell
Proofreader: Karin Waldhauser

First edition: October 2023
Deposit copy in Switzerland: October 2023

Bergli is being supported by the Swiss Federal Office of
Culture with a structural grant for the years 2021–2025.

Bergli

TABLE OF CONTENTS

Schnitzelbängg

St. Moritz

INTRODUCTION

Switzerland is a country. I have been living here for the past 12 years and I, for one, am almost entirely convinced of its existence. In this book, I have assembled the components of this mysterious, linguistically convoluted nation and described them from my outsider perspective. Alphabetically organized between **Aare** and **Zytglogge** you will find answers to the following questions:

- Where and when am I at most risk of being attacked with **confetti**?
- What is a **Bourbine** and should I be offended when the **Romands** call me one?
- If I'm anticipating being arrested on corruption charges, which hotel in **Zurich** should I stay in?
- What are 11 different possible meanings of the phrase **En Guete**?
- What on earth is a **Schümli Pflümli**?

Now, you might be asking yourself, who are you and why should I trust you? Well, I am a Canadian who speaks **Swiss German** every day and knows how to play the **alphorn**. I have spent hours mastering the meticulous Swiss art of bundling paper for **recycling**. I have come in 13th place at a **Jass** tournament. And I have eaten cheese fondue on more than one occasion.

Judge my qualifications as you will. But keep in mind what the famous Swiss comedian **Johann Schneider-Ammann** said: *"Rire, c'est bon pour la santé"*. Laughter is good for your health.

Aare

The longest river to run entirely within Switzerland. Consists of melted glacier water, so jumping in it can sometimes cause you to shriek "Aaaaaaaaare!".

Absinthe

An alcoholic spirit invented in Val de Travers in Neuchâtel and subsequently banned for almost a hundred years. The ban was lifted in 2005 after Switzerland realized that the whole green fairy thing was a myth and it was no more hallucinogenic than other alcoholic spirits. Absinthe had been brewed in secret in Val de Travers during its ban and some producers regret it going legal, because it had been so much more fun to break the law.

Advertising

They say you can tell a lot about a country by looking at its advertising. Well, I don't know if "they" say it, but I just did and I'm the person writing this book.

Advertising in Switzerland uses a lot of **Swissness**. **Cows** are everywhere, even if they have nothing to do with the product. Swiss flags. Alpine meadows. Traditional dress. **Roger Federer** pops up with alarming regularity. Swiss German plays an important part, even to the extent of awkwardly dubbing over German actors in television spots.

Moreover, many things considered to be typically Swiss have their origins in advertising. (See **Globi**, **Gian and Giachen**, **Figugegl**.)

And then there's political advertising, but we'll talk about that later. (See **political advertising**.) (That's how this book works.)

Airing

There are two kinds of Swiss. Those who have the compulsion to constantly open the windows to let healthy fresh air in and those who are compelled to close them again because of a perceived "unhealthy" draft. This fundamental ideological

disagreement between these camps has surpassed abandoned coffee cups and loud phone calls as the main source of conflict in the Swiss workplace.

Aldi
German supermarket chain with many stores in Switzerland. As a foreign interloper it needs to put even more emphasis on having Swiss products than **Migros** and **Coop** and its **advertising** reflects this. Sometimes it tries too hard.

If you were to flip through an Aldi flyer and take a shot of Zuger Kirsch every time you see a Swiss flag, you'd hit the floor before the end of the first page of the meat sales.

Alpabzug
This is a cow parade. Because if there's one thing cows love, it's being in a parade. Preferably while wearing an enormous bell. And having flowers bound to their heads, of course.

Alphorn
Musical instrument designed to be particularly difficult to carry into the mountains, which is coincidentally the place where it is most often played.

Älplermagronen
Macaroni and cheese with potatoes. Traditionally eaten with fried onions and apple sauce. There is some controversy about eating the apple sauce separately or on top of the macaroni. I would advise researching your audience, gauging the atmosphere in the room and identifying an escape route before stating a preference.

Alps
Chain of mountains that makes up 58% of the Swiss landscape and 97% of the Swiss identity. (See also **Swissness**, **advertising**, **spiritual national defence**.)

Also
Universally accepted signal of a desire to end the conversation in German-speaking circles.

Amis
In the French-speaking part of Switzerland, these are friends. In the German-speaking part, they are Americans. Whether or not these are the same people depends on what kind of Americans you know and if they have recently mixed Switzerland up with Sweden.

Anglicisms

English words that have managed to creep into the Swiss vocabulary. Depending on your age, you find this to be evidence of the decline of Swiss civilization or *voll nice*.

AOP – *Appellation d'Origine Protégée*

"Protected designation of origin."

There are 25 Swiss products that are so Swiss that only the version made in that particular geographic area is allowed to carry the name. Among them are, *Zuger Kirsch*, Sbrinz, **St. Galler Bratwurst**, *Tête de Moine* and *Bloder-Sauerkäse*.

At this point, you should note that "**Swiss cheese**" is not on the list. If you should encounter "Swiss Cheese" anywhere else in the world, particularly in North America, think seriously on if you should consume it or not. If, after deep contemplation, you do decide to consume the item, you are morally obligated to state loudly and clearly "I realize that this cheese is not actually from Switzerland and there is a good chance no Swiss people had anything to do with it" before biting in.

Apéro

An *apéro* is a social event consisting of alcoholic beverages and snacks. It can be convened for many occasions, including, but not limited to: getting engaged, leaving a job, starting a job, having a birthday, Christmas, a Friday, a funeral, a wedding, a new apartment, signing a book contract, team building, a Thursday, the end of the work day and if you just feel like it.

There are strict rules involved in an apéro. Guests are all to be greeted individually by name (see **cheek kisses**), glasses need to be clinked while maintaining intense eye contact (see **cheersing**) and snacks must be of the salty, crunchy variety.

The *apéro* is an essential part of Swiss society. It is the grease that keeps the wheels turning. It is the glue that keeps the pieces together. It is the cheese that keeps the mouse happy. It is an opportunity to get to know the Swiss in their natural state. That state being, of course, slightly tipsy with chip crumbs on their collars.

Appenzell

Mountainous canton containing at least three old men who really don't want you to know their cheese secrets and some other old men who still don't think women should have the vote.

Apples

The sworn enemy of **William Tell**. Well, you know, other than that **Gessler** guy.

Apple cider

In Switzerland, apple cider is generally alcoholic. I'm pretty sure **William Tell** had nothing against it.

Après-Ski

The Après-Ski ("after skiing") is a beloved ritual of drinking in a bar on— or in the vicinity of—a mountain. It is important to note that one does not necessarily have to have been recently skiing to participate in the "after ski". Snowboarding, tobogganing or walking ten meters through the snow from the cable car station also counts.

An Après-Ski is traditionally accompanied by **Schlager**, *Schlagrahm* (see **Schümli Pflümli**) and, occasionally, *Schlagen* (fisticuffs, self explanatory).

Aromat

A seasoning mix that the Swiss like to sprinkle over their food. Any proper mountain eating establishment will have it on the table next to the salt and pepper. Aromat tastes vaguely of chicken soup mix and makes everything it touches taste vaguely of chicken soup. It therefore goes best with things that are better when they taste chicken soupy like potatoes or boiled eggs. It tastes terrible on chocolate.

Art Basel

A fancy-schmancy art fair selling fancy-schmancy art to fancy-schmancy people.

Asparagus

National obsession from April to June. Asparagus soup, asparagus omelettes, asparagus *Spätzli*, asparagus samosas. It's everywhere. If you are not fond of asparagus, you can just go back to your home country.

Asylum-seekers

People who cannot go back to their home country and have to pretend to like asparagus.

Auffahrt

"Ascension Day"

A Thursday off work which comes exactly forty days after Easter and should therefore be predictable, but always seems to come as a surprise.

Auszug aus der Betreibungsregister

"Excerpt from the debt collection register"

This is a piece of paperwork that confounds and confuddles expats. Little is known about it other than the fact that one needs it to rent an apartment. To acquire this magical paper, one needs to go to a special office at a special time and ask nicely. It is an epic quest.

Austria

A small country known for its enthusiasm for winter sports, snow-covered mountains and its hard-to-understand dialect of German. So, it's like Switzerland. But with slightly more schnitzel.

START

DER
PAPST HET
Z'SPIEZ
Z'SPÄCK-
BSTECK
Z'SPÄT
BSTELLT.

Bacon cutlery

station), but the stretch a little further down closer to **Paradeplatz**. This is where you will find the luxury stores. Prada, Tissot, Hermès and Cartier, to name a few. And lines of people eager to become slightly less rich.

Balkonien
This is a fancy way of referring to your balcony. It's funny because *Balkon* is balcony in German and adding the "ien" ending on it makes it sound like a country. So when you say you're vacationing in *Balkonien* it sounds like you're going somewhere exotic, when you're really just hanging out with your half-dead petunias. Top notch humour, really.

Bacon cutlery
Something that doesn't really exist, but Swiss people like to talk about the Pope ordering it (too late) while he was in Spiez, because the resulting sentence is really difficult to say in Swiss German. And things that are difficult to say in Swiss German are inherently funny for Swiss German speakers. (See **Chuchichästli**.)

Badenfahrt (See *Volksfest*.)

BAG
This is not a bag, this is the Swiss health department. That's a mistake you only make once.

Bahnhofstrasse
There are over five hundred streets named "Bahnhofstrasse" in Switzerland. However, when one refers to Bahnhofstrasse, one generally means Bahnhofstrasse in Zurich. And not the part of Bahnhofstrasse located next to the *Bahnhof* (train

Banking secrecy
The old Swiss tradition of not snitching on tax evaders. A bunch of outsiders ruined the whole thing by wanting criminals to pay for their crimes.

Barry

A dog responsible for the rescue of 40 people in the mountains before his death in 1814. To honour him, his remains are on display in the Bern Natural History Museum. Please note, if I save 40 lives, I just want a street named after me.

Base jumping

One cannot have as many magnificent mountains and cliffs as Switzerland without attracting lunatics bent on jumping off them.

Basel

A Swiss city bordering both France and **Germany**. Known for its green trams, statue of a tired-looking **Helvetia**, and the **Roche Towers**. One advantage to living here is being able to do your grocery shopping in a country that isn't Switzerland. (See **High price island**, **cross border shopping** and **money**.)

Basic human decency

Letting the people on the bus exit before you board.

Basler Fasnacht

Carnival celebrations that involve political statements on enormous lanterns, high-pitched flute music and the distinct possibility of drowning in *Räppli* "**confetti**". (See also: **Mehlsuppe**, **Morgestraich**, **Schnitzelbängg**.)

Basler Leckerli

A slightly disappointing cookie. This is possibly due to the fact that by the time you get to eating the tin you got as a present for Christmas, they have all gone stale. You should probably put the chocolates aside next time.

Baur au Lac

Fancy hotel in downtown **Zurich**. Should you be arrested on corruption charges while staying there, the friendly staff will hold bedsheets up to hide you from the press photographers.

Bears

Bears feature prominently in Swiss heraldry, but fare rather poorly out in the wild. A bear sighting in Switzerland is rare enough to be headline news, but the unfortunate creature generally ends up being labelled a threat to the populace and shot.

Bern

The capital of Switzerland, but also not the capital of Switzerland because no one bothered to declare it so in the constitution. Officially, it's the "federal city". Known for the slow dialect of its residents and keeping bears in a pit.

Betriebsferien
"Company vacation"
The reason your favourite restaurant is closed exactly the day that you're hungry.

Betty Bossi
A fictional chef that helps you decide what to cook. Despite being based on Betty Crocker, a similarly fictional American, Betty Bossi is considered to be the expert on Swiss cuisine. This idea was somehow not shaken by the fact that her recipes often called for margarine instead of butter. (See also **fictional characters**.)

Bicycles
Preferred mode of transportation for city-dwelling hipsters. (See **Critical Mass**.) German-speaking Swiss refer to them by their French name, *Velo*,

in order to confuse visiting Germans.

Biellmann Spin
A figure skating move made popular by Swiss world champion Denise Biellmann. It involves grabbing the blade of your skate and pulling it up behind your head in a split while spinning around on the other foot. I do not recommend attempting this yourself and accept no liability for injuries caused.

Big Canton, The
This is the Swiss nickname for **Germany**, Switzerland's biggest trading partner. The German-speaking Swiss have a complicated relationship with their big neighbour to the north. They shop there. They watch German television and know their celebrities. They follow German politics. Germany, however, does not return the favour.

Perhaps because of this, the Swiss consider Germans to be loud, impolite and arrogant. Above all, the Swiss hate it when Germans describe Swiss German as "cute". This is unforgivable.

Bilingualism

In a country with four official languages, being bilingual is no longer particularly impressive. Sorry, Canada.

Billag

The company formerly charged with collecting fees for the public broadcaster, **SRF/RTS/RSI**, among others. Billag made grown men afraid to answer their own front doors, for fear that a Billag inspector would come by, see that they owned a television and force them to pay the Billag fee. Although it was recently replaced with the less intrusive, but equally annoying **Serafe**, the collective trauma associated with Billag has left an indelible mark on the Swiss psyche. Please text before you drop by.

Bircher-Benner, Maximilian Oskar

The Swiss doctor who invented **Birchermuesli**. He was slightly obsessed with vegetarianism and a raw food diet. Unfortunately for him, he was born about one hundred years too early to be an Instagram influencer.

Birchermuesli

Switzerland's gift to the world of breakfast. Consists of engorged oats, mangled apples, raisins and other things that are far too healthy for you.

Birthday cake

In Switzerland you are expected to bake a cake on your birthday for other people. One more reason not to tell anyone that it's your birthday.

Bise

This natural wind phenomenon is actually unique to Switzerland, unlike the **Föhn**. The Bise blows from the northeast to the southwest. The mountain ranges in Switzerland act as a funnel bringing dry air in summer and moister air in winter. **Geneva** gets particularly hard hit and the spray from the lake can make cool-looking frozen structures near the lake. The perfect conditions for a spontaneous rendition of "Let it Go". Or at least I thought so.

Bisse

Canals built along cliffs. These are a tremendous feat of engineering that brought water to mountain crops. Many people died during their construction. And now you can hike alongside them, while reading informative plaques and taking pictures for social media.

Blue Balls
A music festival that no one consulted an English native speaker about before naming.

Bobo, DJ
A baker from Aargau who came to fame around the turn of the millennium by yelling "chihuahua" at rhythmically appropriate moments.

Bolz
A dialect spoken in **Fribourg** which is a mix of **Swiss German** and **French**. The dialect is slowly dying out—which is a shame, because it's even better than **Romansh** at totally confusing vast swathes of the population.

Bonaparte, Napoleon
Famous French conqueror who is responsible for a lot of what makes Switzerland Switzerland. (See **Helvetic Republic**, **CHF**, **Congress of Vienna**.)

Böögg
Snot
A glob of mucus originating in your nose. Fun to flick out of windows.

Böögg
Snowman
A wooden snowman with fireworks stuffed inside his head. The Böögg gets burned in a public square in Zurich in order to frighten off the winter. How long it takes for the head to explode supposedly predicts how good the weather in the summer will be. Past performance has shown that it is not particularly good at this, but everyone likes exploding things, so the tradition goes on every year. (See **Sechseläuten**).

Böötle
Clinging to some kind of inflatable flamingo, pizza slice or donut and floating down a river. Often with a beer in hand. Especially popular on the **Aare** in **Bern** and the Limmat in **Zurich**.

Bourbine

This is a slightly derogatory term that the French-speaking Swiss use for the German-speaking Swiss. But the *Bourbines* don't know this, so shhhh!

Bread

Platform for cheese.

Bridge Day

The day between a public holiday and the weekend. For example, the Friday after **Auffahrt**, which is a Thursday off in Switzerland. You could book it off and give yourself an extra long weekend, but only if you beat your coworkers to it. However, that's not going to happen. They already booked it off. No matter how early you email your boss about it, someone else has already done it. It's an eternal mystery.

Brown sugar

The primary source of strife between expats and local Swiss. This is a fundamental, recurring problem in translation, because the Swiss consider raw sugar (*Rohzucker*) to be brown sugar and don't accept that "brown sugar" is a different kind of sugar that's not widely available in Switzerland. Don't bother debating it with them if you value your sanity.

Brünig-Napf-Reuss Line

A geographic boundary dividing Switzerland east of which one plays **Jass** with Swiss German playing cards and west of which one MUST play with French (standard) playing cards. Or else. It is less well known than the **Röstigraben**, presumably because it sounds less delicious.

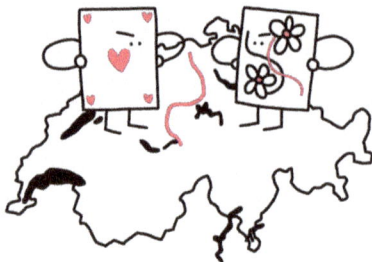

Bündnerfleisch

The most hilarious form of dried meat known to humanity. The mere mention of it can cause uncontrollable fits of laughter in politicians giving otherwise serious speeches to parliament. Well, at least it happened that once. But once is enough to go viral worldwide and secure a place in Swiss internet history.

Bunkers

For decades, buildings in Switzerland were required to include air raid bunkers where citizens could shelter in the case of a nuclear attack. These rooms are now tasked with the noble purpose of protecting empty tv boxes, spare sheets and old ski boots from the threat from above.

Bünzli

Close-minded being embodying all of the worst stereotypes about the Swiss. They're a stickler for rules, a hater of foreigners, a sprinkler of **Aromat**. In foreign lands they can be found complaining about poor service and late trains.

Typical *Bünzli* activities include:

- Reporting your neighbours for putting out their recycling on the wrong day.
- Watching that car with the loud stereo idling outside your apartment building with suspicion from behind your white curtains.
- Being personally proud of the Swiss franc going up in value against the Euro.
- At the movies, sitting in your assigned seat, even though it's right next to the only other people in the theatre.
- Saying "If doing these things makes me a *Bünzli*, then I'm proud to be a *Bünzli*".

Bürgerort

The Swiss are technically not citizens of Switzerland, but of their *Bürgerort* "home place" within Switzerland. This home place is not necessarily where they were born. And also not necessarily where their parents were born. It is where their ancestors are from. On their father's side. At some point. The existence of the *Bürgerort* on Swiss passports mostly serves the purpose of confusing border control officers all over the world.

Business hours

The only time that the Swiss Air Force is available to respond to threats. Please be considerate and schedule your attacks accordingly.

Bünzli

Café Crème

The standard cup of coffee in Switzerland. A *Café Crème* is bigger than an espresso, but smaller than a cappuccino. This means it doesn't fit standard takeaway cups and tourists are often confused when they are given a seemingly half-full cup. The crème part doesn't refer to actual cream, but instead the golden froth that forms when the water is forced through the extractor. So tourists are confused again when they have to add cream themselves.

All in all, it's a reasonably good cup of coffee. Try to remember that when you see the bill.

Canton

Instead of states or provinces, Switzerland is divided into 20 full cantons and 6 half cantons. Depending on how you look at this, it means that there are either 26 or 23 cantons. It can be argued either way, so you have two chances to get it right in the citizenship interview.

Capuns

Inverted dumplings. The dough is on the inside, the vegetable is on the outside. And then drowned in cheese sauce because Switzerland. And bacon. Bacon has to be involved somehow.

Caquelon

Essential kitchen equipment in any Swiss household. Customarily used for the preparation of a meal consisting of melted cheese and stale bread (see **Fondue**), the vessel is also useful as a hat, if you have an unusually large head.

Wash immediately after use or be prepared to spend more man-hours than it's worth to clean it. Unless you were using it as a hat. Then it will probably be easier to clean. One hopes.

Cat ladders

Improvised structures intended to allow cats to climb up to upper floor apartments. This is proof that raccoons are not a problem in Switzerland.

Cat wash
A form of superficial bathing that does NOT involve licking yourself. I repeat, do NOT lick yourself when someone suggests you do a quick cat wash. It is NOT appropriate.

Cats
Dinner in Appenzell. Well, it's not a widespread tradition, but there's enough truth to the cat-eating myth that we're still allowed to make jokes about it.

CERN
That place with the thing that could create a black hole, crushing all of humanity within its immense gravity in the blink of an eye. Starting with Geneva. Sorry, not sorry. (See **Geneva**.)

Cervelat
Switzerland's national sausage. Can be made into a salad.

Cervelat-Promi
"Sausage Celebrity"
B- or C-list celebrity. *Cervelat-Promis* in Switzerland include influencers, former Miss Switzerlands and television hosts. They cannot be made into a salad.

CH
The abbreviation for Switzerland. Obviously. (see **Confoederatio Helvetica**.)

Chalandamarz
On the first of March, young boys march around **Graubünden** ringing enormous bells in order to scare off the winter. Don't worry, girls get to participate too! They get to make the paper flowers that decorate the bells. That's surely just as much fun.

Chaplin, Charlie
An Englishman who lived in Switzerland for 25 years. In Vevey, there's a Charlie Chaplin statue, a Charlie Chaplin museum and Charlie Chaplin chocolates shaped like shoes that were designed in his honour. And they say the Swiss don't like expats …

Chasperlitheater
Puppet show for kids that promotes violence against crocodiles.

Château de Chillon
One of the most ridiculously scenically located castles in the world. Really, really, really ridiculously good looking.

Cheek kisses
An appropriate form of greeting in many social circles in Switzerland. These come in sets of three. Two is too few. Four is too many. Five is right out.

Cheersing

Cheersing is the most obvious English translation of the German word *Anstossen*. The word is not often used in anglophone countries, because cheersing is not as important an act as here. But English speakers charged with describing the elaborate ritual as it exists in Switzerland need an equivalent word in English and are therefore forced to say cheersing until the word echoes through your brain.

Cheersing is an elemental part of an **Apéro**. One must clink glasses with what other cultures may consider to be an excessive amount of people. Several times per evening. Slightly exaggerated eye contact is very important during this ritual and surprisingly not considered to be creepy.

In the German-speaking part of Switzerland *Prost* is the typical toast, but feel free to try out *Santé*, *Viva*, *Salute* or **Chuchichästli**.

Cheese

Coagulated cow juice. Tastes delicious on bread.

Cheese-sausage salad

Salad made out of sausage and **cheese**. Really, I'm not sure what you were expecting here.

CHF

Switzerland's national currency, Swiss francs. Before the **French** invaded in 1798 and proclaimed the **Helvetic Republic**, each **canton** had its own currency. Today we have a unified currency with fun, coloured bills with illustrations of hands on them. Thanks, **Napoleon**.

Chindsgibändel

Fluorescent sashes that children wear. This theoretically allows adults to see the children from a distance and safely avoid them. However, the sneaky devils can swarm a city bus within seconds. Nowhere is safe.

Chocolate

The essence of life. Chocolate is considered a Swiss specialy despite the fact that the raw materials have to be imported from far-away countries.

The Swiss are responsible for inventing milk chocolate. The Belgians invented pralines. Which one of these is more important depends on your personal preferences and if you've recently bit into a cherry cream (ew).

Chocolate side (*Schoggisiite*)

This is your best side for photos. Probably best if it's not literally smeared with chocolate while you're posing.

Cholera

In Valais, this is not a virulent bacterial disease, but instead a delicious pie containing potatoes, apples, leeks and cheese. But it could also be the disease. Depends on the context. Be careful out there.

Christ child, the

An invisible being that brings presents to children on Christmas Eve. This entity is literally supposed to be the actual Christ child. Why Jesus is hanging around Swiss family homes in the form of a child two millennia after his death as an adult is a question no one wants to ask. Probably because they like getting presents.

Christmas markets

In late November and early December, Christmas markets start popping up all around Switzerland. They are packed with overpriced goods, high-calorie snacks, **mulled wine** and way too many people. The general Christmas cheer just barely manages to edge out the vague feeling of being ripped off.

Christmas season

As Halloween is not as widely celebrated in Switzerland, stores see no reason to wait until after October 31st to start stocking Christmas paraphernalia. According to some unsettling reports, poinsettias have been sighted as early as the first week of September.

Chuchichästli

The Shibboleth of Swiss German. The word means small kitchen cupboard, but functions more like a code word. Only those who pronounce it correctly are considered successfully integrated. The Swiss take great joy in hearing foreigners saying it wrong and slightly less joy in hearing them say it correctly. Either way, it's guaranteed entertainment for two minutes.

Church bells

Depending on if you have ever lived in an apartment next to a church, these are either a quaint European tradition or a torture device designed to taunt your insomnia at 3:15 am.

Church tax

If you confess to the Swiss authorities that you have a religion, then you have to pay the dues. The dues being the church tax. But only if your religion is one of the few recognized ones. Jedi is fortunately not one of them.

Cigarettes

The reason people will sometimes come up to you on the street to ask you if you have fire, making you feel vaguely like Mowgli from *The Jungle Book*.

Circus Knie

Known as "Switzerland's national circus". Named for the family and not the location of the bruises on the acrobats.

Civil courage

The courage to stand up for what you believe in for the betterment of society. This may involve snitching on garbage tourists. (See **fee bags**.)

Civilian service

Young men who refuse to do military service because they are unrepentant pacifist hippies are allowed to do "civilian service" instead. This means they basically take a break from their regular job to go do another unrelated job.

Cleanliness

The Swiss are extremely clean. Except when it comes to cigarette butts, graffiti or the walls in public stairwells.

Confetti

Weapon of choice for children at various folk festivals around the country. (See **Basler Fasnacht**, **Luzerner Fasnacht** and **Zibelemärit**.) Should you be the victim of an attack, you are doomed to find confetti in your pockets and the seams of your winter coat for decades to come.

Note: Do not pick confetti up off of the ground to throw back and do NOT use the word "confetti" in **Basel**. It is *Räppli*. Even if you are speaking English. Trust me on this.

Confoederatio Helvetica

The Latin name for Switzerland as found on its coinage. This is used instead of writing out the name of the country in all of the official languages: *Schweiz*, *Suisse*, *Svizzera* and *Svizra*. This is the one time in history that Latin was the least complicated option.

Congress of Vienna (1815)

A meeting where a bunch of foreigners determined a great deal of the things that make Switzerland Switzerland.

The five Great Powers of the time (**Austria**, Britain, Russia, Prussia and **France**) decreed that Switzerland should be neutral. This was to create a buffer between post-Napoleon France and Austria. In order to be an effective buffer, Switzerland was obliged to maintain an army to defend its borders.

These borders were also decided upon in this meeting. This was when **Geneva** joined the confederacy and the land between Geneva and the rest of Switzerland just had to come along for the ride.

Consensus addiction

This is the Swiss characteristic behind their democratic system, their social interactions and even their manner of speaking. In comparison to their German counterparts, Swiss-German speakers use the conditional tense almost compulsively. Swiss political parties are forced to work together to govern the country. Conflicts in everyday life must be solved as amicably as possible. It's cute, when it's not annoying.

Coop

Large Swiss retailer. Land of the **Coop children** and competition for the **Orange Giant**.

Coopkind/Migroskind

Other countries have the Crips and the Bloods. Switzerland has Migros-kids and Coop-kids. One does not choose a side, one is born to a side. Either your parents shopped at Migros or they shopped at Coop. This endowed you with a number of characteristics as described by Swiss comedian Gabriel Vetter in a generation-defining stand-up sketch.

German retailer **Aldi**, feeling left out of this divisive tradition, started a campaign to include Aldi-kids in the menu of gang choices. This surprisingly had some success.

Cowbells

An acoustic warning device prevent-

ing large 600 kg mammals from sneaking up on unsuspecting hikers.

Cows

Large, 600 kg mammals responsible for more human fatalities than sharks are. Worldwide. I suppose this wouldn't be as impressive if we limited the statistic to Switzerland. Shark attacks being exceedingly rare in Switzerland.

Crèmeschnitte

A layered pastry designed to be difficult to eat unless you buy expensive special equipment. (*Crèmeschnitte* scissors are a thing.) Luckily, it still tastes delicious even when the crumbs are all over the table and the cream is smeared across your face.

Creux du Van
Switzerland's Grand Canyon. A huge, horse-shoe-shaped indentation in the landscape located in Neuchâtel.

Do not get too close to the edge, no matter how cool the photo would look. Dying while taking a selfie is the ninth most embarrassing way to go.

Critical Mass
A mass bike ride occurring on the last Friday in each month in various cities in Switzerland and around the world. **Zurich** in particular has thousands of participants. If you need to cross the road when Critical Mass is passing by, it just might be better to rethink your plans for the evening.

Cross-border shopping
As goods are cheaper in neighbouring countries and borders are mostly open, many Swiss do their shopping in **Germany**, **France** or **Italy**. In **Basel** this just involves walking down the street or over the bridge. Be careful how much meat you buy, or the customs officer will get you. (See **Customs**.)

Crossbow
A weapon that was invented in China. Coincidentally, a crossbow is part of a "Swiss made" logo that indicates that products were not made in China.

Cuckoo clocks
A German invention that Orson Welles falsely attributed to Switzerland. In the film *The Third Man*, he opines that Italy's history of bloodshed produced Michelangelo, Leonardo da Vinci and the Renaissance, while Switzerland's peaceful history of brotherly love produced the cuckoo clock.

As the cuckoo clock is a Bavarian invention, I humbly suggest the quote be corrected to say that "500 years of peace and democracy" in Switzerland produced the **Robidog**.

Culture shock
The feeling that tourists get when paying for their *Café Crème* in **Zurich**.

Customs
The people who will stop your car at the German border and ask to look at your sausage. (See **cross-border shopping**.)

Decheler

Decheler

People who collect coffee creamer lids. Yes. Those little bits of plastic or foil. This is a thing in Switzerland.

Diglossia

A fancy word that describes the use of two different languages for different situations within the same community. So, when the Swiss speak **Swiss German** to their friends at recess and **High German** to the teacher in class, they're engaging in diglossia. Same thing when they text Swiss German, but write an email to the same people in High German. You should bring this up to them if you want to be considered a *Klugscheisser*.

Dinner party

An event at which you should arrive exactly on time and bring a present of chocolates, flowers or wine. It is a great sign of friendship to be invited to a Swiss person's house. Don't screw it up.

Direct democracy

A defining feature of the Swiss government is its direct democracy.

This system brings the Swiss to the polls at least four times a year to vote on issues as varied as tax reform to cannabis legalization. Participation is generally low and a quarter of the population aren't allowed to vote.

"The people have the last word" is a noble principle, but when the Swiss vote against giving themselves six weeks of holiday every year, one becomes seriously disappointed in one's fellow citizens.

Dorffest (See *Volksfest*.)

Doodle

An online tool to help find an appropriate time and date when all of the participants are available. It's very helpful in organizing and coordinating people according to time. Possibly the most Swiss thing to be invented in Switzerland.

Double accordion bus

Type of public transportation that subtly undermines your confidence in floors.

Dreikönigstag

"Three Kings Day"
January 6th. A day on which you should regard any baked good you are offered with suspicion. It could contain raisins.

Drinking age

In Switzerland, the drinking age is 16 for beer and wine and 18 for spirits. Though to be honest, children have had wine mixed into their **fondue** since they were toddlers, so I'm not sure why they bother with the official age.

Drinking fountains

Free-flowing drinking fountains are abundant in Switzerland. Many of them look simply decorative, so tourists are a bit flummoxed when they see the locals drinking directly from them. (See **tap water**.)

Dunant, Henri

A Swiss businessman who let his trading company run to the ground because he got distracted by the idea of saving countless millions of lives. (See **Red Cross, the**.)

Dürrenmatt, Friedrich

Acclaimed Swiss playwright and novelist who famously called Switzerland a prison in his speech: "Switzerland—A Prison".

Double accordion bus

federal constitution laid out the federal system of democracy that we know today. (See **Federalism**, **Direct Democracy**). But there was no secret meadow and no nifty hand sign, so it's just not as cool as the **Rütlischwur**.

Einstein, Albert
Famous Swiss citizen. And we will not be arguing about that.

Emmentaler
The classic hard, yellow, Swiss cheese with holes in it. The holes in the cheese are produced by the gaseous emissions of the bacteria used to create the cheese.

The name "Emmentaler" has not been origin protected (see **AOP**), despite the **Swiss Cheese Union**'s best efforts. "Emmentaler" was already being produced all over the world by the time the union existed and could therefore no longer be copyrighted.

Gaseous emissions, after all, happen everywhere.

En Guete
A phrase often heard at meal times. The Swiss will tell you it means "Enjoy your meal", but that barely scrapes the surface of this complicated expression. In various contexts it can mean:

"Hello."

"Goodbye."

"Can I also be a part of this conversation?"

Easter
That time of year when you take a boiled egg, hold it gently, but firmly in one hand, find someone who is also holding a boiled egg gently, but firmly in one hand and hit their egg with your egg. Whoever's egg cracks, loses. It's called *Eiertütschen* (egg hitting). This is even funnier when you know that *Eier* is also the slang word they use in German for testicles.

Edelweiss
A small, hairy flower which has gotten a little out of hand as a national symbol.

Eidgenosse
"Confederate"
Direct descendant of **William Tell**. This is quite difficult to manage, because William Tell is a fictional character.

Eighteen-forty-eight
1848 was the year of the founding of modern Switzerland, when the

"I see that you are about to eat and I don't want you to think I am rude."

"May I eat now?"

"Yes, we can eat now."

"Look, I can be Swiss too."

"Why are you eating something at your desk in between meals?"

"You had better like this rösti. I spent five hours slaving away in the kitchen for this."

"You forgot to say *En Guete* to me."

"Where did you get those cookies and can I have one?"

So if you're confused about what to say, say "*En Guete*". At the very least, that will make the person you're talking to confused as well.

Engadin

Part of the canton of Graubünden known for its spectacular fall colours, nut pie and king. (See **White Turf**).

Engadiner Nusstorte

Pecan pie with a lid and walnuts instead of pecans. Keeps for quite a while and as such makes a good take-home souvenir from **Engadin**. If you subsequently forget to unpack it from the bottom of your suitcase, the next summer it makes an excellent, deadly, throwing discus.

English

Switzerland's unofficial fifth language. Over 5% of the population speak it as a mother tongue. This is ten times more than **Romansh**, which IS an official language. When Swiss people from different language regions converse, they often do it in English. Nonetheless, you are to frown slightly if you hear it on the tram.

Escalade, L'

A failed attempt by the Duke of Savoy to conquer Geneva in 1602. The Catholic invaders were thwarted by one Catherine Cheynel, who dumped a cauldron full of boiling vegetable soup on them and raised the alarm. Every year Genevan children smash chocolate cauldrons filled with marzipan vegetables to celebrate the death of their enemies.

Europe

Despite its best efforts, this is still the continent on which Switzerland is located. (See **European Economic Area**, **European Union**.)

European Economic Area

A free trade zone incorporating the **European Union**, Norway, Iceland and **Liechtenstein**. Switzerland is the hole in the middle of this donut. The voters of Switzerland—against the wishes of the federal council and parliament—refused membership of this economic partnership in a 1992 referendum. It was considered to be a step towards joining the EU, which would have put Switzerland under "**foreign judges**", despite all that the (fictional) **William Tell** went through (or not) to save us from exactly that fate.

European Union

Switzerland's neighbour on all sides, except for **Liechtenstein**. Switzerland has a complicated relationship with the European Union, consisting of many convoluted bilateral agreements.

The EU is Switzerland's biggest trading partner and the two share many of the same democratic values. This makes it more difficult to demonize, but not impossible. (See **foreign judges**.)

Eurovision Song Contest

Switzerland has not won the Eurovision Song Contest since Celine Dion won it for them in the 80s. That's right, the famous Canadian singer. She won it for Switzerland. Just thought you should know.

EXIT

Swiss company known for killing old people. Professionally and consensually.

Expat

Due to the prevalence of **English** in certain workplaces, foreigners can live in Switzerland for years without learning a local language or making friends. It is exactly this group of people who are branded with the label "expat". Less privileged newcomers are known as immigrants. Whether or not they have any friends depends to some degree on their willingness to repeatedly say "*Chuchichäschtli*".

Expat bubble, the

An air-tight enclosure that can only be penetrated with passive-aggressive Google-translated Post-it notes.

False friends

Words that are spelled the same in two different languages, but have completely different meanings. Also the reason German speakers are wary of accepting a *Gift*.

Fasnacht

Carnival. A Catholic festive season celebrated before the fasting time of Lent. This differs from canton to canton and community to community. The most famous versions in Switzerland are **Basler Fasnacht** and **Luzerner Fasnacht**. If you don't live in either city, don't venture an opinion on which festivities are better. You'd be risking your life, no matter what you say.

Zurich, a traditionally Protestant canton, does not have city-wide celebrations. However, the random presence of **confetti** on the streets in springtime points to the likelihood of you having just missed some kind of parade.

Federalism

A form of government in which responsibilities are shared between the national and regional (in Switzerland's case, cantonal) governments. This can lead to conflicts, when, in one far-fetched example, neither government wants to take responsibility for imposing restrictions during a pandemic.

Federal Council

The executive branch of the Swiss government. The council is made up of seven politicians from several different political parties in proportions dictated by a "magic formula".

The federal council members are chosen by the Swiss parliament after a night of much political wrangling called "**the night of the long knives**." No long knives are actually involved, but we can't rule out the possibility that a few politicians are carrying **Swiss Army Knives**.

Despite coming from parties across the spectrum of Swiss politics, Swiss Federal Councillors are forced to agree with each other in public. This is called the collegiality principle and it is a credit to the Swiss character that no councillor has exploded from the repressed rage and murdered any of their colleagues (yet). That we know of, of course.

Federer, Roger

The most overused face in Swiss **advertising**. It's a good thing that he's the greatest tennis player of all time, otherwise he'd be just another sell-out influencer.

Fee bags

Official garbage bags. Household waste is only to be disposed of in these designated bags. The costs of garbage collection are included in the price of the rather expensive plastic bags or in some municipalities in normal bags affixed with rather expensive stickers. Infringers who put garbage out in normal, unmarked bags will be hunted down by **garbage police**.

The introduction of this system of garbage collection happened slowly in different municipalities over the last few decades, often leading to "garbage tourism", where people would drive over to the next town where fee bags had yet to be implemented and deposit their household waste there.

The system of rolling the costs of garbage collection into the price of the bags has resulted in an increase both in recycling and complaining about it. The only hold-out in all of Switzerland is **Geneva**. In this bastion of freedom, garbage collection is paid for by taxes and residents are allowed to use whatever bags they want.

Fête des Vignerons

The Swiss have long held to the idea that a festival seems much more special if it doesn't happen every year. Zürifäscht happens every three years and Badenfahrt happens every ten years. The citizens of Vevey have taken this principle to the extreme and have a wine festival that occurs every quarter century or so. This ensures that the young drunk people at one festival are middle-aged drunk people by the next and nostalgia has properly blurred the memories of the last festival by the time the next one rolls around.

FIFA

This is the *Fédération Internationale de Football Association*. Or, as that translates in English: Bunch of corrupt asshats.

Fictional Characters

Made-up people are the building blocks of the Swiss identity. (See **William Tell**, **Helvetia**, **Heidi**, **Osman**.)

Fifth Switzerland, the

This term refers to the Swiss people that live outside of Switzerland. These people often have Swiss citizenship and can vote, despite perhaps never having lived in the country themselves, possibly not speaking any of the official languages and, for all we know, not liking **Aromat**.

Figugegl

This seemingly random collection of syllables sounds like something that the Swiss came up with to bamboozle

foreigners who had thought that they had finally gotten a handle on Swiss German, but is actually a short version of the phrase *Fondue isch guet und git e gueti Luune*. "Fondue is good and creates a good mood". It was originally an advertising slogan, but now has imprinted itself on the Swiss psyche and can be heard around **caquelons** to this day.

First of August

Switzerland's national day. Usually celebrated with fireworks, bonfires and small, round loaves of bread with tiny paper Swiss flags stuck in them. The flags make the bread taste more patriotic.

Five Decilitres

The appropriate serving size for beer. This is half a litre, for those of us who use millilitres and litres, but just can't get used to those pesky values in the middle.

Five Franc Coins

These have one of the highest face values of any circulating coin in the world. More importantly, having a pocket full of them makes you feel like you are hoarding pirate treasure.

Five Rappen Coins

As **SBB** ticket machines don't take them, they're a useless weight in your pocket. They may be shiny and gold coloured, but only foreigners think they're cool.

FKK

If you see a sign with these letters on it, you might want to avert your eyes. Or take off all of your clothes. One or the other.

Flag juggling

Sport/art form consisting of hurling a flag into the air. Competitions require you to stand inside a circle while doing it. Like many things in Switzerland, there are penalties for stepping outside of the lines.

Flamingos

Not native to Switzerland, but can often be seen floating down the

Limmat or the **Aare** carrying drunken Swiss. (See **Böötle**.)

Föhn
A hairdryer that comes over the mountains and blows dry air into the valleys.

Folk Festival (See **Quartierfest**.)

Folk Music
Swiss folk music includes **yodelling**, **alphorns** and accordions. In other words, all things you shouldn't practice in your apartment. I learned that the hard way.

Fohrler Live
"Jugend und Gewalt – ich schlage zu"
People often talk of making "television history". My friends, this episode of a live talk show about youth violence in 2001 is Swiss television history. Protagonists from the show are still being interviewed about their appearances twenty years later, the most famous being "Osman", a violent youth who considered his "honour" to be worth defending with his fists.

The hour is packed full of young men who boast about beating up people for looking at them askance. Women who call them to account are subject to sexist jokes. Many of the absurd, self-aggrandizing statements that pop up in the show have made it into the cultural lexicon of Switzerland. A sample:

"Jede chan mache was er will, will jede staht dezue was er macht." Anyone can do what they want because everyone stands behind what they do.

"Meinsch du bisch krass will du Bändäli hesch?" You think you're tough, because you have a bandana?

"I bi Spanier, wennd mi bi dä Rasse wotsch nenne." I'm Spanish, if you want to name me by my race.

The Swiss find these quotes absolutely hilarious and repeat them at every opportunity—even decades later. At this point, I suspect the problem is not that the Swiss don't have a sense of humour. It's more that the humour is a little too specialized to be understood by your average foreigner.

Fondue
Fondue was transformed from a regional specialty to a national dish when the **Swiss Cheese Union** wanted to sell more cheese in the 1930s. What better way to get rid of surplus dairy than to convince people to eat buckets full of it?

The traditional recipe involves multiple types of cheese (see *Moitié-Moitié*), wine, cornstarch, garlic and kirsch. The hardened leftovers stuck to the bottom of the *caquelon* are considered to be the best part. (See **Grossmutter**.)

These days, fondue has become such a fundamental part of Swiss culture that the proper preparation of fondue is a question that comes up on citizenship exams. I've always said that too much studying is bad for your health.

Fondue season

Fondue is an exclusively winter dish for locals and the retailer Coop announces fondue season every year with its advertising campaign titled "It has to stink a little." The only people you'll find eating fondue in the summer are the tourists and the seriously cheese-addicted.

Foreign judges

The boogeyman of the Swiss. Originally this was the **Habsburgs**, but these days it generally refers to the **EU**. The Swiss even refused to be a part of the UN until 2002, despite hosting the European headquarters in **Geneva**.

"Foreign judges" are what the fictional **William Tell** was fighting against. The Swiss really, really don't want foreigners deciding their laws.

Foreign workers

They do, however, want foreigners to work for them. Switzerland imported many foreign workers to build its railways. Particularly Italians. They were expected to trot off home afterwards, but as it often happens, many did not. (See *Saisonnier*.)

Foreigners

Over a quarter of the population of Switzerland consists of "foreigners". Switzerland, however, does not automatically grant citizenship to people who are born in the country. So many "foreigners" are actually Swiss-born, local-language-speaking, fondue-loving *Bünzlis*.

Four-person-compartment

The appropriate number of occupants of a 4er compartment on a train is one. If you're forced to share the compartment with someone else, then Switzerland is letting too many immigrants in.

France

The second most popular holiday destination for the Swiss. Also a popular place for **cross-border shopping**. The Swiss have mostly gotten over the time that **Napoleon** invaded Switzerland. Mostly. **Bern** still wants its state treasure back.

Français fédérale

French as spoken by German-speaking politicians. Generally consists of using French words, but German grammatical structures and a strong German accent. Simultaneously mocked and appreciated by the French-speaking population, because as ridiculous as *français fédérale* sounds, at least the politicians aren't speaking **Swiss German**.

Frauenfürze

Literally "women's farts", these are firecrackers. Children quite enjoy playing with them in the streets. Despite these female farts sounding exactly like gunfire, they rarely cause panic in Swiss cities. (See **gunshots**.)

Freedom

Being allowed to drink a beer by the lake without having to conceal it in a paper bag.

French

The mother tongue of 22% of the Swiss population. (See **Romands**, **Romandy** and the **Röstigraben**). The French spoken by the Romands in Switzerland is similar to the French spoken in France with just a few notable **Helveticisms**. This ensures that if you speak perfect Swiss French, Parisians will still be snotty to you.

French goodbye

Leaving without dawdling about announcing the fact that you're leaving. Basically, the opposite of Brexit.

Fribourg

A city that's so excessively bilingual that some residents mix **French** and **Swiss German** in the same sentence. (See *Bolz*.)

Friends

One of the top complaints of **foreigners** in Switzerland is that it is difficult to make friends with the Swiss. It is true that the Swiss tend to be withdrawn and guarded amongst strangers and stay friends with the people they grew up with. But there's always the possibility that they just don't like you personally.

Frisch, Max

Famous Swiss author of many novels and plays, including *Switzerland without an army? A Palaver*. He was way more critical of Switzerland than I would ever dare to be.

Frontalier

Someone who works in Switzerland, but lives just across the border in one of the neighbouring countries. They get the benefits of a high Swiss salary without having to pay the high Swiss cost of living. Also known as clever bastards.

Frustration

The feeling you get when you hold in your pee on the train, because you'd rather use a toilet that's not in motion, only to realize that you have to pay to use the ones at the station. Either you hold it in for another hour or you give in to corporate greed. It's a pity we're all too civilized to pee on the tracks out of spite.

Füdlitrycheln
"Butt ringing"

The practice of binding a cowbell to your backside and walking around ringing it.

Fussball
"Soccer"

22 grown men chasing a ball around a grassy field for 90 minutes in order to make sure that the local riot police can justify their purchase of a water cannon.

Garbage police

GA

Riding public transportation in Switzerland is most satisfying when you don't have to think about how much money you're spending on it. The best way to do this is to buy a GA (*General-abonnement*) once a year, try to forget about its price and blithely pop on and off of trains, buses and boats all over Switzerland without having to pay for tickets each time.

Gallicism

This is the term for **French** words that have crept into another language. **Swiss German** is absolutely riddled with them, but people don't seem to be as bothered by them as **anglicisms**. It could be because French words have a certain *je ne sais quoi*, but I think it's a little more undefinable than that.

Garbage police

Special investigators who go through improperly discarded garbage and look for clues to finding the owners. These vile perpetrators will be fined for their wrongdoings. Their wrongdoings being, generally, not using the appropriate plastic bags. (See **fee bags**.)

Garbage shark

Yes, Switzerland has **garbage police** AND garbage sharks. The latter, however, are far less frightening. The name refers simply to the public trash cans in **Zurich**, whose silver shape vaguely resembles a shark.

Garbage tourism (See **fee bags**.)

Geneva

Home to the UN, the International **Red Cross** and the longest bench in the world. The rest of **Romandy** tends to disown it, considering the residents to be arrogant and un-Swiss. However, in my opinion, when one's city has the longest bench in the world, one is allowed to be a little arrogant about it.

German

It is often claimed that over 60% of the Swiss population speak German as a first language. The Germans would beg to differ. (See **Swiss German**.)

Germany (See **Big Canton, The**.)

Gessler, Hermann

Habsburg bailiff whose fixation on having people bow to his hat kicked off the entire **William Tell** epic. The lesson here is not to place too much importance on headwear. You could inspire the foundation of a new country and get yourself assassinated.

Giacobbo/Müller

A long-running sketch show which appeared on **SRF** featuring, surprisingly, comedians named Giacobbo and Müller.

Gian and Giachen

Two mountain goats (*Steinböcke*) from a particularly successful **Graubünden** tourism campaign who enjoy taunting mountain bikers from their rocky perch. The short spots reached cult status in Switzerland.

In recent years, Gian and Giachen have gone the way of many internet personalities and have started selling merch and NFTs.

The NFTs are called "Bockchain".

Giger, HR

Famed Swiss artist who designed the alien in the movie *Alien*. He has his own rather creepy museum in

Gruyères. It's the least Swiss thing you can imagine.

Gipfeli
"Little summit"

A *Gipfeli* is the Swiss version of the croissant. It has a little less butter and is therefore drier. French-style croissants can also be found, generally labeled as *Buttergipfeli*. There are also *Schoggi-Gipfeli* (chocolate-filled *Gipfeli*), *Laugengipfeli* (lye-dipped *Gipfeli*), *Nussgipfeli* (nut-filled *Gipfeli*), *Schinkengipfeli* (ham *Gipfeli*) and *G20-Gipfeli* (intergovernmental forum comprising 19 countries and the EU).

Glacier

Ancient mass of compacted snow that has solidified and shaped the landscape with its enormous weight. A glacier is always much further away than it looks and contains more corpses than you think.

Glacier Express
The slowest "express" train in the world. The Swiss are very proud of it.

Globi
Beloved advertising mascot turned children's book character. Has a beak like a parrot, but appears to be covered in blue skin instead of feathers. Wears magic shorts that always show an even pattern, no matter what direction you look at them from or what angle his legs are at. If you should see a train car bearing his image, do not ride in it, unless you're fond of shrieking children.

Gnomes of Zurich
An old, derogatory term for the bankers of **Zurich**. I can assure you that the bankers of Zurich are people just like you and me. Except they can afford to go to the bars near **Paradeplatz**.

Gold
There's definitely gold in Switzerland. How much and where it comes from, we don't like to talk about. (See **Banking secrecy**.)

Gold coast
The shore of Lake Zurich that gets the glorious, golden evening sun. The name definitely doesn't come from the rich people that live there. Definitely not. The other side with less sun is known as the *Pfnüselküste* "sniffles coast".

Golden Egg, the
The ugliest hotel in Switzerland. It is a massive, gold-coloured, only-vaguely-egg-shaped luxury hotel in Davos.

Gopferdamminomal
"God damn it again"
The better in-word than **Chuchichästli**. Only someone truly integrated will blurt out "*Gopferdamminomal*" after accidentally stepping in a cow patty.

Gotthard Auto Tunnel
A popular place to hang out in your car on the Friday before a holiday weekend. It must be fun, because people spend hours there. Just sitting in their cars. Barely moving …. Weird. But hey, to each their own. (See **Ticino**).

Graffiti
A popular way to express your devotion to a **Fussball** team, your hatred of cops and your bad English grammar.

Graubünden
Large **canton** known for its mountains, three official languages and

talking mountain goats. (See **Gian and Giachen**).

Grisons

The former English name for **Graubünden**. Which happens to also be the **French** name for Graubünden. It only makes sense that the English would use a French name for a canton full of **German**, **Italian** and **Romansh** speakers.

Grittibänz

Sweet bread baked in the shape of a man, traditionally eaten on December 6th. It's best not to stare into their bloated faces for too long. Just bite the head off before they threaten to haunt your dreams. They're no good stale.

Grossmutter

Can be either a layer of hardened **cheese** (see **Fondue)** or a kindly old lady.

"Grüezi mitenand!"

When heard on **public transportation**, this phrase means: "You AND your dog better have a ticket or else you're about to be publicly shamed." Or possibly: "Hello, everyone". But more often the former.

Grüezini

A slightly derogatory term that people from **Valais** have for people who say "*Grüezi*" (i.e. people from **Zurich**).

Gruyère

Famed Swiss cheese that has been named the world's best cheese FOUR times at the World Cheese Awards. We're not crying, you're crying.

Gschwellti

A Swiss dish consisting of boiled potatoes and cheese. This is entirely different from **Raclette**, which is also a Swiss dish consisting of boiled potatoes and cheese. To say otherwise is to invite derision, disappointment and possible deportation.

Guetzli
"Cookies"

This book is not really meant to be a **Swiss German** dictionary, but this word is included here just to make sure that any expats who might be reading this never miss out on an opportunity to eat Swiss cookies. *Guetzli*. You can thank me later.

Guggenmusik

Pop music adapted to be played by marching bands. The fact that it's played slightly out of tune is not a bug, but a feature. The louder, the better. The jangling, off-tune tones of Madonna and the Backstreet Boys are meant to scare off the winter. And, as winter does seem to disappear at some point after **Fasnacht** every year, I suppose it works.

Guns

There are many guns in Switzerland. Men in military service often take theirs home with them so that they will be ready to fight invaders at the drop of a hat. The hat should take its time hitting the ground, however, because ammunition will still be stored at central depots.

Gunshots

The sound of gunshots is not to be feared in Switzerland. More likely than not you're just passing by one of the many shooting ranges to be found here. If you're in the middle of a city, it's probably just women's farts. (See **Frauenfürze**.)

Halberd

Habsburgs

Austrian monarchs that ruled vast swaths of Europe between 1273 and 1918. They came into conflict with the Swiss many times during that era. (See **Rütlischwur**, **Morgarten**, **Sempach** and **William Tell**). The Swiss hated the Habsburgs so much that they invented Switzerland in self-defence.

Hahnenburger

Not a burger. Not even close. *Hahnenburger* is a Swiss German term for tap water. And Switzerland has good **tap water**. Very good tap water, you might say. But if you're expecting a burger, you're destined for sadness here. Sigh.

Halberd

Traditional Swiss weapon. A Halberd is a long pole with an axehead and a spike. The backside of the axehead is a hook, with which infantry can pull mounted knights down from their horses. This is a more effective tool for killing than a **Swiss army knife**, but slightly more difficult to fit in your pocket.

Halbtax

A discount card from the **SBB** that gets you half price on public transportation tickets. It keeps the locals happy. Because if they had to pay the prices the tourists do, Switzerland could have a full-scale riot on its hands.

Half-Canton

The cantons of **Basel**, Unterwalden and **Appenzell** were each split into the half-cantons of Basel-Stadt and Basel-Landschaft, Obwalden and Nidwalden and Appenzell Ausserrhoden and Appenzell Innerrhoden. These half-cantons each have only one representative in the upper house of the federal assembly, while full cantons have two each.

They still have more representatives per capita than **Zurich**, though. Were Zurich to be split into two half cantons, it could be divided into the city of Zurich and Zürcher Oberland, or more appropriately, FCZ and GC fans. (See *Fussball*.)

Health Insurance

There are two kinds of Swiss people. One kind sticks with the same health insurance for life. The other checks which one is the cheapest on a comparison website every year, signs up for it and sends a **registered letter** in November by A Post to cancel their old insurance exactly on time.

Health insurance is mandatory in Switzerland. And so is complaining about it.

Heidi (asteroid)

An asteroid discovered by Swiss astronomer Paul Wild in 1979. He named it after the character. According to the internet, it is not likely to impact Earth and destroy life as we know it. Just in case you were worried.

Heidi (food)

A brand of dairy products owned by the **Orange Giant**.

Heidi (book character)

A gullible orphan who embodies the values of alpine Switzerland.

The *Heidi* books feature an overly romanticized depiction of mountain life, where it never rains, a pile of hay is infinitely more comfortable than a feather bed and even the hum of mosquitos is described as cheerful.

Heidi's naive prattle inspires devotion in nearly everyone she meets, including a conveniently rich benefactor.

In this idyllic portrayal of poverty, a monotonous diet of goat's milk, bread and cheese can cure a wheelchair-bound city girl of her paralysis. Meanwhile, the jealous, wheelchair-smashing "Goat Peter" is rewarded with a weekly stipend for his bad deeds.

The story of Heidi's journey from the mountains to the big city and back has been made into several movies, television shows, computer games and a tourist destination (see **Heididorf**).

Heidi Game

There was one day in history when **Heidi**'s appearance on television screens across the USA inspired rage and indignation.

It was a 1968 American Football League game between the Oakland Raiders and the New York Jets. The last few minutes of the television broadcast were cut off to show a new television movie version of *Heidi*. Viewers completely missed the dramatic turn of events when the Raiders scored two touchdowns in the last minute. Enraged football fans flooded the telephone lines of the broadcaster to complain, actually blowing the switchboard.

Later, the network decided to overlay a graphic showing the result of the game during the film—just as the formerly paralyzed Clara was taking her first dramatic steps. This disruption enraged all of the *Heidi* fans. The "Heidi Game" was voted one of the most memorable games in pro football history.

Switzerland–USA relations have never really recovered.

Heidibrunnen

A fountain near **Heididorf** dedicated to the memory of *Heidi* author **Johanna Spyri**.

Heididorf

A village formerly known as Oberrofels which has been turned into a life-size museum for events that never took place from a novel about a girl named, you guessed it, **Heidi**.

Heidihaus

A house in **Heididorf** that's meant to represent the house that **Heidi** lived in during the winters while she was going to school.

Heidihof

A restaurant/hotel near **Heididorf**. Delicious *capuns* dumplings.

Heidihütte

A hut in the mountains near **Heididorf** that's meant to represent the house that **Heidi** lived in with her Öhi.

Heidiland

A highway rest stop where you have to pay to use the toilets.

Heidiweg

A hiking path that leads from the Heidi-Shop to **Heididorf**, **Heidiweg**, **Heidibrünnen** and back.

Heidi-Zoo

Okay, I made this one up.

Heimatort

Disappointingly not some kind of cake. (See *Bürgerort*.)

Helvetia

A fictional woman, symbol of the nation. Pictured holding a shield and a sword, but wearing long flowing robes that would probably get in the way of using either.

A statue of her in **Basel** depicts her sitting, tired, looking out over the Rhine, her shield, sword and a suitcase sitting behind her. Rather careless of her to leave her bag unwatched like that. In many other cities it would have been stolen. But in Swiss Basel, it's safe behind her. It could be because the Swiss are rich enough not to need to steal. Or it could just be that the thing is bolted to the ground.

Helvetic Republic

Napoleon's short-lived attempt to organize Switzerland centrally like **France**. The system didn't quite work out and after five years was converted back to **federalism**. This was disappointing in some respects, because the name "Helvetic Republic" has a nice ring to it and would definitely not be mixed up with Swaziland.

Helveticisms

Words unique to Swiss use. Often these are words that are shared between the languages of Switzerland.

Swiss German-speakers say *Zucchetti* like the Italians. The Swiss Italian-speakers say *voilà* like the French. The Swiss French say *witz* like the Germans. And **Romansh** is only spoken in Switzerland, so technically the entire language is a Helveticism. They win.

High German

This is an official language of Switzerland, but not the one that the Swiss typically use. **High German** is used for writing, education and politics, but **Swiss German** is used for daily conversations. The Swiss version of High German is also not quite the same as the standard German used in **Germany**.

Almost every Swiss person has a story of speaking their very best High German to someone from Germany and the German thinking that it was Swiss German. This is embarrassing for those it happens to, but funny for everyone else.

High price island

Switzerland is landlocked, but still considered to be an island. Unfortunately, not the fun kind with beaches and piña coladas. It's the kind where everything costs more than in the surrounding areas. (See **cross-border shopping**.)

Hiking

It is almost too easy to go hiking in Switzerland. The country is absolutely riddled with conveniently well-marked hiking routes.

Children are forced to go hiking with their parents. They hate this and stop going as soon as they have a choice. Later in life, it becomes cool again to go with your friends and post pictures of mountaintops on social media. Then everyone's doing it and there's too many people on the trails, so you stop. When you have kids, you force them to go until they're old enough to say no. Even later in life, it's cool again to go in huge gangs of retirees. (see **Wandergruppe**.) It's the circle of hike.

Hiking trails

The natural habitat of **cows**.

Holiday apartments

Short-term rentals in typical holiday destinations like Zermatt or Grindelwald that often come with cute names like Colorado Cottage, Edelweiss Lodge, Chalet Barbara or Maison Belle Taco. Generally have a ski-room, candle-powered raclette grill and kitschy decorations that say "Keep Calm & Love Crans Montana".

Hopp Schwiiz
This means "Go Switzerland!" in the sporting sense. Feel free to shout it at random occasions whenever you see anyone doing anything mildly exhausting.

Hornussen
A traditional Swiss sport. The batter hits the puck with an extra-long, bendy golf club/whip, sending it flying down the field. The opposite team tries to knock it out of the air by flinging pizza-shovels at it. Where exactly they got the shovels and if a pizza is currently burning is a question that is somehow never addressed.

Humanitarian tradition
Switzerland has historically been a safe haven for political refugees and a generous contributor to foreign aid. A Swiss citizen, **Henri Dunant**,

founded the **Red Cross**. The Swiss also export over 100,000 tonnes of chocolate each year.

Idiotikon

An ongoing attempt to document all of the words of **Swiss German** in one dictionary. This is a moving target and has been in progress for over a hundred years. The Idiotikon has 16 published volumes so far. Just because "idiot" is in the name, doesn't mean that it's an idiotic undertaking. Also doesn't mean it's not, though.

Inferiority complex

What the German-speaking Swiss suffer from when listening to Germans speak **German**.

Influencers

In Switzerland, the influencers are always busy showcasing its beautiful mountains, stunning train rides and expensive hotel rooms. It's all very suspicious.

Insanity

Creating the same **Heidi** movie again and again and expecting the story to become interesting.

Insurance

In Switzerland, accident insurance and **health insurance** are two different things and often, two different companies. Because this determines who gets the bill, this can lead to intense paperwork conflicts over whether your broken ankle was an accident or an illness. Make sure you and your shattered bone have your story straight.

Interlaken

This Bernese city located between two lakes is surprisingly called "between lakes". Known for extreme sports, tourists, and waiters who speak English, but not German.

Iodine tablets

Pills that are given out to Swiss households within 50 kilometers of a nuclear power plant. This has the effect of reminding you that you live within 50 kilometers of a nuclear power plant and making you slightly

uneasy every time you're rummag-
ing through your medicine cabinet
and come across the box of pills.

Italian
The mother tongue of 8% of the
Swiss population. Spoken in **Ticino**,
Graubünden, and in **Zurich** by piz-
za restaurant waiters trying to seem
more authentic. (See also **Ticino**,
Polentagraben.)

Italian-speakers
The Italian-speaking minority in Switzerland is often overlooked. I'm afraid
that's also going to be the case here.

Italy
Popular holiday destination for the
Swiss who want a little more adven-
ture than just visiting **Ticino** and/or
want to spend less money.

Italian-speakers

Jass

Switzerland's national card game, traditionally played on a small piece of carpet in teams of two, so that you can always blame someone else when you fail to make enough points.

Sometimes the highest card is the lowest and the lowest is the highest. There are lords instead of queens and banners instead of tens. The game is played counterclockwise instead of clockwise and the cards are dealt three at a time instead of one at a time.

The suits are shields, roses, bells and acorns instead of diamonds, hearts, spades and clubs. Unless, of course, you're west of the **Brünig-Napf-Reuss Line**, in which case you use the French cards. Please always consult a map before taking out your Jass cards.

To sum up, the rules are convoluted, the play is backward, there's a built-in geographical divide and no one quite knows why the whole thing works as well as it does. It's very Swiss.

Jein

A word combining "*ja*" and "*nein*" which is basically just a cop-out, in my opinion.

Jungfraujoch

A magnet for international tourists. Rich international tourists. A return ticket for the ride from the valley to the top of Jungfraujoch costs approximately 200 francs. That people pay this is a testament to the beauty of the area. Or the laziness of humanity. One or the other.

Jura

Switzerland's newest canton, separated from Bern in 1979. The adjective for describing the Jura region is "jurassic". In this jurassic region there happens to be a park filled with life-sized replicas of dinosaurs. This is, of course, known as ... ... Prehisto-Park. What else would you call it?

Kafi Complet

Breakfast for dinner, which would be fine if the Swiss ate a decent hot meal for breakfast.

Kantönligeist

"Cantonal spirit"

The impulse that makes the Swiss mock people who pronounce the word *Erdbeertörtli* slightly different-ly, because they live three kilometers further to the west.

The nation known as Switzerland is actually a confederation of separate cantons. (See **Federalism**.) Things can be quite different between two neighbouring cantons. And I don't mean just the garbage collection practices. (See **Fee bags**.)

The Swiss often identify more with their home canton than with Swit-zerland as a whole. This is kind of like Americans who say they're from Texas instead of from the USA. I rec-ommend, however, not making this comparison to a Swiss person.

Kapellbrücke

The least efficient way to cross the Reuss river. The Kapellbrücke is a cov-ered wooden bridge in **Luzern** dec-orated with historic painted wooden panels. Not only does the bridge cross the river at an angle, it is constantly congested with snap-happy tourists.

Walking over the bridge requires a ninja-like ability to stay out of peoples' photos while also looking grumpy enough not to be asked to take photos of them yourself. Should you need a break in the middle of this harrowing journey, a water tower in the middle is also home to a con-venient souvenir stand. The Kapell-brücke is also occasionally the set of Bollywood films, so watch out for unexpected mass dance sequences.

Katzenzüngli

"Cat tongues"

A specialty in Switzerland. Don't pan-ic, they're just chocolates vaguely shaped like tongues.

Kebab

Classic late night meal for people on the way home from bars. Don't be afraid to ask for "with spicy". What constitutes "spicy" in Switzerland is generally blander than mayonnaise on white bread.

Kelso

A monkey that escaped from Zurich Zoo in 2012. He was assumed to have been killed by the local wildlife or the cold, but his body was never found. For all we know, Kelso found his way into the nearby **FIFA** offices and has been running the place ever since. That would definitely explain a few things.

King of Switzerland

Switzerland does not have a king. It's resolutely against the whole idea of a monarchy. Well, except for the King of Schwingen. (See **Schwing-erkönig**.) And the **Queen of Queens**. And the King of the Engadin (see **White Turf**). And the King of Olten (a dead cat). But, other than that, royalty is looked down upon.

Klugscheisser

Literally, a "smart shitter". A know-it-all. A smart-ass. A wiseacre. Windbag. Smart aleck. Swot. Brainer. Smarty-pants. Nerd. Walking encyclopedia. Pedagogue. Mr. Wise Guy. Clever-dick. Annoying kid at the front of the class. My brother-in-law Matt. Smart-arse.

Knabenschiessen

Literally "boys shooting", Knaben-schiessen is a **Zurich** festival that centres around a shooting competition. These days, the girls are allowed to participate too, but regardless, it's still a party for children with guns.

Knabenschiessen

Landei

Labour Day

In Switzerland, Labour Day is celebrated on May 1st. Whether or not one should work on a day to celebrate workers seems to be a disputed question. Some cantons have the day off. Others have a half day off. In other cantons, just the public sector employees have the day off. In yet other cantons it depends on what municipality you're in within the canton. And some municipalities have the day off, not because of Labour Day, but because of various religious reasons.

   This whole system may seem confusing and convoluted to outsiders, but that's honestly how the Swiss like things to be.

Lake Geneva

The lake on which Geneva is located. In **French**, the name of this body of water is *Lac Léman*. You may also use this **French** name in **English**, if you're trying to suck up to non-Genevan **Romands**.

Lake Luzern

The lake on which **Luzern** is located. In **German**, the name of this body of water is *Vierwaldstättersee*. You may also use this name translated into **English**, "Lake of the Four Forest Cantons", if you want to totally confuse whoever you're talking to.

Landei

Literally "country egg", this is someone who grew up in the country as opposed to the city. There is a historic rivalry between city folk and country eggs, but don't worry, "egg-hitting" still refers to actual eggs. (See **Easter**.)

Landjäger

A dried sausage that is popular with hikers because it doesn't need to be refrigerated. Can also be boiled and served with cheese and potatoes, but that applies to almost everything in Switzerland, so it's barely worth mentioning.

Landsgemeinde

"Cantonal Assembly"

This is an old form of **direct democracy** that is still practiced in the cantons of Appenzell Innerrhoden and Glarus. Here, all of the registered voters gather in the public square and vote on issues by raising their hands like schoolchildren. As you can imagine, anonymity is not particularly supported under these conditions and your neighbour Hans-Peter is going to know exactly how you voted.

If this mass public gathering doesn't sound fun enough, just know that men get to bring their weapons with them. Your gun is considered a form of identification.

Langstrasse
The nightlife district of **Zurich**. Can be slightly seedy at some hours of the night, but is slowly becoming gentrified. You can still get drugs, prostitutes and hot wings here, though, so there's that.

Language
Sociolinguist Max Weinreich said that a language is a dialect with an army and a navy. Apparently having a few speedboats patrolling the border lakes doesn't count. Sorry, **Swiss German**.

Language barrier
Next to **religion**, the **mountains**, the **urban-rural divide**, money and the applesauce-on-or-next-to-the-*Älpler- magronen* question, language is one of the main things dividing Switzer- land. (See **Röstigraben**, **Polentagra- ben** and **Romansh**.)

Large Hadron Collider (See **CERN**.)

Lausanne
The only city in Switzerland that has a metro system. Suck it, **Zurich**.

Liechtenstein
Liechtenstein is to Switzerland what Switzerland is to **Germany**. When you're used to being the little broth- er, sometimes you forget that you're also the big brother to someone else. If the Swiss can't tolerate Ger- mans making jokes about them, then they shouldn't make fun of the Liechtensteiners.

It is, however, very tempting. It is very convenient for the Swiss that there is an even smaller, richer alpine country that allowed women the vote even later than the Swiss did at the national level (1984).

The principality of Liechtenstein uses **Swiss Francs** and has no military. In the event of an invasion, it's hoping that the Swiss will protect it. The Swiss have said "no dice" because they're neutral but said they would be willing to protect their own territory while standing on Liechtenstein and may- be that would end up being the same thing. Liechtenstein is very small.

Lindt
Manufacturer of fancy chocolates known the world over. The found- er invented the process that makes chocolate into the smooth confec- tion we know today. Possibly Swit- zerland's greatest contribution to the world. Well, except for maybe the **Red Cross**. Or **Einstein** .... No, I'm going to go with chocolate. I swear it's not because I'm hungry.

Locarno
Not the same city as **Lugano**.

Lugano
Not the same city as **Locarno**.

Luxemburgerli
A confection bearing a startling similarity to the French macaron. However, they are clearly different and better. And more expensive. But also better. Just accept this as a fact.

Luzern
Scenic city coincidentally located on **Lake Luzern**. Beloved tourist destination known for a covered bridge (see **Kapellbrücke**), a statue of a dying lion and particularly drunken *Fasnacht* celebrations.

Luzerner Fasnacht
Carnival celebrations that involve waking up at 4 a.m. in order to start drinking at 5 a.m., a rain of shredded paper and throwing sticky teabags at the ceiling of a bar.

Language barrier

Marmot

M

colder months of the year. They make an excellent hand-warmer while waiting for the bus. It's a shame about the taste.

Mass immigration
The boogeyman of the right-leaning Swiss. (See also *Überfremdung*.)

Matter, Mani
Berner best known for singing about matchbooks, parking meters and arranged marriages. He was a certifiable genius.

Matterhorn, the
Gravity-defying hunk of rock and renowned chocolate label model.

Mehlsuppe
Soup made out of flour traditionally eaten at **Basler Fasnacht**. The most unlikely satisfier of drunken hunger in the world. But hey, what works, works.

Märkli
Sticker collecting for adults. Ostensibly, one accepts this strip of stickers at the grocery store check-out for the potential discounts, but the real joy is in peeling them off one by one and sticking them in the little booklets. Pure satisfaction.

Migros (See **Orange Giant**.)

M-Budget
The generic brand of **Migros**. Known for its slogan "We're young and need the money." Spends a surprising amount of money on advertising for a brand that's supposed to be cheap.

Mandatory military service
Military service is mandatory for young men in Switzerland. Unless they are deemed unfit. Or they decide they don't want to do it. (See **Civilian Service**.)

Marmot
Alpine groundhogs. A common sight in the **Alps** and in gift shops, where you can find a yodelling, dancing variety. Definitely gift these to your friends who have kids. They will love you for it. The kids. Definitely not the parents.

Marroni
Roasted chestnuts. These are available from small stands during the

Milizsystem

"Militia system"

The principle of "don't quit your day job" when you go into politics, fire-fighting or armying. Politics, however, has become more and more complex (In Switzerland! Shocking!) and fewer and fewer parliamentarians are able to keep their other job while politicking.

Minarets

A form of architecture that was banned in Switzerland after a referendum in 2009. Apparently some tower shapes need political intervention.

Moitié-Moitié

The standard cheese formula for fondue. Half **Gruyère**, half Vacherin Fribourgeois. Also a cheesy metaphor for the melting pot of cultures in Switzerland.

Money

Something that the Swiss quite like to have, but don't like to talk about.

Money laundering

The Swiss are known for their **cleanliness**.

Morgarten, the battle of

An important battle in the history of Switzerland. In the winter of 1315, troops of the allied cantons Uri, Unterwalden and Schwyz ambushed and defeated the numerically superior **Habsburg** cavalry. The Swiss took no prisoners, brutally slaughtering the Habsburgs and forcing many to flee into the lake where they drowned in their heavy clothes and armour. **Hopp Schwiiz**!

Morgestraich

An elaborate joke that people from **Basel** play on visitors from Zurich to get them to wake up inhumanely early in order to start drinking at four in the morning. They've been doing this for hundreds of **Fasnacht** seasons now. Baslers are really committed to the bit.

Monkeys

Despite monkeys not being native to the country, journalists who ask unwelcome questions are considered to have been bitten by them. How this happens remains an unresolved mystery. Zoos generally report on these kind of escapes. (See also **Kelso**.)

Montreux

Ridiculously scenic town known for its jazz festival, recording studio, Freddie Mercury statue and being the inspiration for one of the most famous guitar riffs of all time. Said riff is from Deep Purple's "Smoke on the Water" and it goes like this: Dun, dun, DUUUN, dun, dun, DA-DUUUN, dun, dun, DUUNN, DUH-dunnnnnnn.

Mountains

The defining feature of Switzerland. They provide a strategic military retreat (see **Reduit**), a tourist attraction (see **Skiing**) and a place for **cows** to stare at hikers.

Mountain cable car

What's the use in having gorgeous mountain panoramas if only a handful of ultra-fit climbers get to see them? The **Alps**' panoramic beauty have been made accessible to all. Well, to all the people who have enough money to buy a cable car ticket.

Mountain hut

The traditional mountain retreat for the traditional Swiss family. Generally under some kind of heritage protection, so that renovations don't disturb the quaint look of the Swiss countryside. Liveable ones are almost impossible to buy, so your best bet is to marry into a family that has one. Tip: Turn on Tinder while hiking in the mountains.

Müesli

This **Swiss German** word has made it into the English Merriam-Webster dictionary. The word is the diminutive form of "*Mues*" (purée). Too bad the rest of the world pronounces it like "*Müüsli*" (small mouse). Brings a whole new meaning to breakfast.

Mulled wine

If you could distill the Christmas spirit into a beverage, mulled wine would be it. It's sweet, intoxicating, and ruins your white mittens.

Multilingualism

A Swiss person speaks at least four languages fluently. In most cases, this would be **Swiss German**, **German**, **English** and *français fédérale*.

Never trust the Swiss when they say they can only speak English "a little". They are far more articulate than you, a native speaker. In addition, they are probably capable of ordering a coffee in another five languages.

Naked hiking

The previous national anthem had the same tune as the British one, which led to several embarrassing situations in the 20th century, so Switzerland went with the psalm until they could come up with something better.

They never came up with anything better.

National Sport of Switzerland

Depending on who you ask, this is either **Schwingen**, **Jass** or **cross-border shopping**.

Nazi Gold

The Swiss are sorry about that whole thing, really.

Nestlé

One of Switzerland's biggest companies. According to Reddit, it's evil. Mostly because of their attempts to privatize drinking water in developing countries. But they also make a lot of chocolate so they can't be all bad. Right?

Newspaper

Newspapers in Switzerland are crucial to the functioning of society. Firstly, you can hold them in front of you to maintain an illusion of privacy from the other people in your four-person train compartment. You can also put them under your feet if you have that four-person compartment to yourself and you want to put

Naked hiking

A mythical cultural tradition supposedly practiced in **Appenzell**. They must not have mosquitos in Appenzell.

Nati

This is the nickname for the Swiss National Team and generally refers to the men's soccer team. To the untrained ear, the pronunciation of this word in Swiss German sounds a lot like "Nazi". Which means the untrained tongue should probably avoid using this nickname. You'll want people to know exactly which group of zealous young men you're cheering for.

National anthem

The Swiss national anthem is the "Swiss Psalm" a song that was only picked provisionally. On **the first of August** the text is handed out so that people can sing it together because the average Swiss only knows the first two lines off by heart.

your feet up. Most importantly, they also provide a sturdy frame for the loose single papers in your bundle of paper recycling. Oh, and you can read them, I guess.

Neutrality
A convenient excuse to not get involved in tricky arguments like what land belongs to whom.

Nicholas of Flüe
Also known as Brother Klaus, Nicholas of Flüe was an influential mystic in the 15th century who left his wife and ten children to become a hermit and is now the patron saint of Switzerland.

On the 13th of May, 1940, just as Switzerland was preparing for the possible Nazi invasion, a glowing hand appeared over Waldenburg, near the German border. The manifestation was interpreted to be the hand of Nicholas of Flüe, protecting Switzerland from war. It gave hope to the Swiss in their dark hours and was dubbed "The Miracle of Waldenburg". This is not to be confused with "The Miracle of Bern", which was just a soccer game.

Night of the long knives
In Swiss politics, this is the night before new federal councillors are chosen by the Swiss parliament. Much politicking goes on. Very little stabbing.

Nicholas of Flüe

OLMA

One thousand franc note
The second most valuable circulating bank note in the world. Brunei's 10 000-note beats it out. I know the Swiss are disappointed with that, but you can't be the best at everything.

Openair Festival
Opportunity to throw off oppressive Swiss expectations of **cleanliness** and be loud, drunk and slightly smelly.

Official Languages
Switzerland has four official languages and they're damn proud of it. **Multilingualism** is a core value of Switzerland. Mostly because it sets them apart from the Germans, the French and the Italians. But not all at once.

Language plays a huge part in the national identity as well as in the identity of subgroups within Switzerland. It is always fun to have a secret code that other people don't understand and in this competition, the **Romansh**-speakers are winning.

Orange Giant
This is not a mythical Swiss monster, but instead the largest Swiss grocery chain and the largest Swiss employer, **Migros**. They are particularly proud of the fact that they don't sell alcohol. Pronounce the S in Migros if you want to sound like a foreigner. (See also **Coopkind/Migroskind**.)

Osman
Iconic tragic/comic figure in Swiss television history. (See **Fohrler Live**.)

OLMA
The annual fall agricultural festival in **St. Gallen**. Functions primarily as a place for politicians to have photo ops with barn animals. (See *Volksnah*.)

Ovomaltine
Known better in the rest of the world as Ovaltine because of an ancient spelling error, Ovomaltine is a Swiss drink that doesn't help you do anything better, but helps you do it for longer. Supposedly.

ON shoes
A Swiss brand of running shoes generally worn by people who are not currently running.

Panoramaweg

Panettone

Christmas cake of Italian origin also beloved by the Swiss. And it would be fine if there were no raisins in it and if it didn't get completely stale by the time one got to get a piece from the work break room. However, under these circumstances it is an abomination of nature.

Panini Cards

Tradable soccer stickers. I advise against eating them.

Panoramaweg

A hiking path that takes longer to hike on account of all of the photo breaks.

Papa Moll

A popular Swiss children's book series. The titular character is an accident-prone father with exactly five hairs on top of his head—an important detail that was completely disregarded in the live action movie adaptation. For this reason, I refuse to watch it.

Papierlischwiizer

"Paper Swiss". Derogatory term for people with Swiss citizenship who are for some reason not considered to be real Swiss. That reason is generally racism.

Paradeplatz

The banking district of **Zurich**. This is where you can find the stereotypical Swiss in suits. Apparently they don't like to be called **gnomes**.

Paragliders

Tiny, colourful specks in the sky above **Interlaken** that briefly make you think that the aliens are finally invading.

Patriotism

Many Swiss are very proud of being Swiss. They think that Switzerland is the best country in the world. And they don't like being told they sound like Americans when they say this.

Pepita
Although "pepita" in English is a pumpkin seed, here it means a Swiss grapefruit-flavoured soft drink that has a parrot as a mascot. I guess you can't use **cows** for everything.

PET-Recycling
Not the recycling of house pets, you monster. This refers to the recycling of PET-plastic, generally drink containers. Pets go to doggy heaven.

Pfadi/Scout de Suisse
The Swiss boy/girl scouts. That place where Swiss youth learn that peeing on campfires is the appropriate way to put them out. The boys, at least.

Pick-me expat
A foreigner who has overdone the whole integration thing and has become more Swiss than the Swiss. This person puts **Aromat** on their **raclette**,

plays **alphorn** in the **mountains**, has mastered the art of **Jass** and is the only one wearing a Swiss flag t-shirt at the *Public Viewing* when the *Nati* gets eliminated in the quarter finals of the European Championship. (See the author of this book.)

Pinkelpause
This is a pee break. Most movie theatres in Switzerland will provide one in the middle of a film. Evil tongues suggest that the break is to sell more popcorn, but I like to think that it exists because *Pinkelpause* is a fun-sounding word.

Planetenweg
"Planet walk"
A scale model of the universe, which requires one to hike from planet to planet. This emphasizes how vast space is and how tiny the floating rock we call Earth is. There are at least 24 of these planet walks in Switzerland. The Swiss must like to be reminded how insignificant we all are. Or they just are running out of ideas for themed hikes.

Platzspitz aka "Needle Park"
Part of Zurich next to the main train station where drugs were openly consumed for years before it was cleaned up in the nineties. This is a fun fact to tell visiting relatives who think Switzerland is just mountains and cheese.

Polentagraben

The **Röstigraben**'s lesser known counterpart in the south. This is the linguistic barrier between German-speaking Switzerland and Italian-speaking Switzerland. I suspect that whoever was in charge of making these names up was carb-loading. Possibly before the Zurich Marathon or a speech in parliament.

Politeness

Wishing the call centre employee "*einen schönen Abend noch*" even though they interrupted your favourite show with their unsolicited call and you secretly think they are the scum of the earth.

Political Advertising

Political campaigns in Switzerland are fought most visibly through colourful political posters. Complex topics like pension reform or factory farming practices are reduced down to simple, short sentences and colourful images. "Bread Monopoly: No!" "Constitutional Road Network Project: Yes!" "Women's suffrage? No!"

"Direct Federal Taxation: Yes!" "Stop bratwurst discrimination!"

If this seems superficial and infantilizing, that's because it is. But that's how politics works all over the globe. Should we really make fun of the Swiss for it? Yes, we can!

Popular initiative

An instrument of **direct democracy** that allows ordinary citizens to propose a change to the Swiss constitution. For it to go to a vote, the initiative needs to have 100,000 valid signatures. Popular initiatives of the past include: the Messenger Pigeon Initiative, the ban on Freemasons and the abolition of vivisections.

The vast majority of popular initiatives do not pass.

Post

At the post office in Switzerland you have the choice between sending your letter A Post (first class) and B Post (second class). A Post is for the people who really mean it. (See **Bünzli**.) B Post is for the weak of resolve, who secretly hope the letter never arrives.

PostBus

Where the train doesn't go, the Post-Bus goes. The yellow buses have a distinctive honk, which you can hear as they defy the laws of physics on narrow, twisting, alpine roads. They also have wifi, which is a very nice, modern convenience that it would be great to also have on trains. If this hint is not obvious enough for you, here it is again: **SBB**, please install wifi on your trains.

President of Switzerland, The
The presidency rotates between the seven people on the Swiss **Federal Council**, so that anyone who ever learns the name of the Swiss president is already wrong about it the next year.

Pretzel Sandwiches
Beloved form of sandwich made out of a soft pretzel sliced lengthwise. It's like a sandwich with windows, so you can see what you're getting into. And what you're getting into is butter everywhere, because that's what oozes out of all of the holes. Commonly eaten on trains, where greasy fingers are slightly more of a problem than usual.

Pseudo-anglicism
Words and phrases that look like **anglicisms**, but are not actual **English** words used in that way. Some **German** examples would be: *Handy*, *Beamer*, and *Peeling* (cellphone, projector and scrub). This generally is only a problem when German-speakers attempt to use the words with their German meaning in English and invite their American friends to a *Shooting*. (See also **false friends**.)

Public holidays
These vary according to canton and district. The disparity often leads to internal Swiss **cross-border shopping**. For example, the Catholic parts of the canton of Aargau have the Feast of Corpus Christi (60 days after **Easter**) off and the shops are closed there. However in neighbouring Protestant **Zurich**, everything is still open. That means Aargauers with the day off work can flood the shopping malls of Zurich, where the poor suckers are working as normal.

Public transportation
This is the most under-appreciated national infrastructure. Invisible if it works. A cause for great tribulation if it doesn't.

In one television advertisement, a visitor to the country listens to an **SBB** announcement apologizing for a three-minute delay. He finds it quite funny that the train operator would bother asking for forgiveness for such a trifle. Passengers used to Swiss punctuality however, find this completely appropriate. Three minutes late is unacceptable. Nine minutes is cause for a riot.

Public Viewing

A public event where people watch something on television together. Generally a sporting event like a World Cup soccer game. Not to be confused with a "viewing", which in anglophone countries generally means the viewing of a dead body before a funeral.

Punctuality

The Swiss compulsion to take an extra lap around the block so that you don't arrive at your meeting more than thirty seconds early.

Puttitschiffra

This means bra in **Valais German**. It has been named as a favourite word by some prominent Valaisians. However, the people of this region pride themselves on the obscurity of their dialect, much as the Swiss do on a grander scale when dealing with people from **Germany**. And if too many people know what *Puttitschiffra* means, it's not fun anymore. They'll likely have to make up another word for it. I suggest Businator.

Quartierfest (See **Dorffest**.)

Quantum of Solace
The best James Bond film ever, because one of the villains briefly speaks Swiss German in it. The moment where a henchman named Elvis tells his mother on the phone that it's hot brings indescribable joy to the Swiss. This overshadows every other James Bond scene featuring Switzerland and even Ursula Andress's turn as a Swiss Bond girl.

Queen of Queens
The Queen of Queens lives in Switzerland. There is a new Queen of Queens every year and she earns her title by fighting the other queens. She pushes her head against the other queen until it backs down. The Queen of Queens is a cow. I possibly should have mentioned that first.

Quiet hours
Noise restrictions extend from ten in the evening to seven in the morning and also include a few hours at lunchtime despite the fact that Switzerland doesn't have a siesta tradition. And of course all day **Sunday**. Despite a persistent myth to the contrary, you ARE allowed to flush the toilet during this time. Probably.

Quantum of Solace

Raclette Oven

Raclette

The perfect Swiss meal for people who can't cook. If you can boil potatoes, you can make raclette. The dish involves melting raclette **cheese** and scraping it on top of or next to the aforementioned boiled potatoes. Typically served with pickles and pickled onions. If you're feeling particularly shameless, you could have it on bread instead of potatoes. You rebel, you.

Raclette Oven

A device for the melting of individual slices of raclette cheese in little trays. Sausages and vegetables can be grilled on top. This is standard kitchen equipment in a Swiss household. During the winter it lives on the dining room table, where it is always somewhere in the process of heating up, cooling down or drying off after being indifferently washed.

Recycling

An elaborate ritual which involves separating green from brown glass, a mystical garbage tram and the tying of precise packages with string. This occurs according to a strict timeline as decreed by the sacred garbage calendar. Those that fail to perform this elaborate dance with perfect precision will be threatened with Swiss disapproval. Or possibly the **garbage police**.

Unlike Christianity, this religion shall not be practiced on **Sundays**. That would be illegal.

Red Cross

International humanitarian organization founded by Swiss businessman **Henri Dunant**. Red Cross workers are identified by a red cross on a white flag. As the **Swiss flag** is a white cross on a red flag, this has led to many people mistaking official Swiss establishments for first aid stations. A thorough education in first aid is therefore recommended for Swiss diplomats all over the world.

Red Passport, The

The Swiss Passport. A great national treasure that must be guarded at all costs. (See *Überfremdung*.)

Reduit

"The National Redoubt"

Switzerland's defence plan during World War II. If the Nazis attacked, the plan was to retreat into the mountains, defend the **marmots** and abandon the lowlands. This would allow them to keep control of the highly valuable mountain passes and defend their position more easily. The populated lowlands were considered to be expendable. Sorry, Olten.

Referendums

Switzerland's national pastime. (See **Direct Democracy**.)

Rega

A mountain rescue service with fancy helicopters. The Rega most often comes to mind as you stumble in the quickly fading sunlight on your way down one of Switzerland's mighty mountains.

Hmm … you'll think to yourself. Maybe I should have signed up for a Rega membership … Maybe I should have taken a left at that fork in the path back there … Maybe I shouldn't have used up the rest of my phone's battery making a time-lapse of the clouds passing in front of the mountain peak. Oh, was that a **cowbell** *I heard? Where exactly was the last sign I saw? They would probably come rescue me anyway, right? I wonder how much it would cost as a nonmember …*

At this point, however, you've spotted the **PostBus** stop and are saved, not to think about Rega until the next time you're in a bit of a tough spot on a mountain and are contemplating your own mortality.

Registered letter

The weapon of choice in dealing with Swiss bureaucracy and in covering your own ass in several paperwork situations. Dispute with your landlord? Send a registered letter. Cancelling an automatically renewing membership? Send a registered letter. Choking on a *Rahmtäfeli*? Heimlich manoeuvre. A registered letter will not help you here. Why did you even think that might help? Honestly …

Reichenbach Falls

The location in Bernese Oberland where Sherlock Holmes finally defeated his archenemy Professor Moriarty and briefly died himself. There is a plaque there commemorating the fictional event, because this was the most exciting time that Switzerland was mentioned in international fiction. Well, except that time someone spoke Swiss German in a Bond film. (See **Quantum of Solace**.)

Reitschule

A much graffitied area near the main train station in Bern. Home to activists, occupiers and annoyingly loud skateboarders.

Religion (See **Recycling**)

Rhine Falls

The biggest waterfall in continental Europe. I advise getting as close to it as is safely possible in order to drown out the sounds of the tourists complaining about the fee they had to pay to walk around there.

Ricola
A Swiss herbed throat lozenge that is irrevocably intertwined with images of **alphorns** and costumed men shouting "Ricolaaaaaa!" These ads ran internationally for many years. So all over the world, when people think of Switzerland, they think of **alphorns** and costumed men shouting "Ricolaaaaaa!"

Is this a good thing? Well, it's better than people remembering Switzerland as that place that the Nazis kept their gold.

Rigi
Location of the first cog railway in Europe. Its construction hailed a new era in the transportation of couch potatoes to scenic mountain tops.

Rivella
Only the Swiss would think to make a sugary, carbonated soft drink out of milk byproducts. Vegans should steer clear of this stealth dairy product.

Robidog
A Swiss invention. It's a combined bag dispenser and garbage bin for the disposal of dog waste. Not the most innovative thing in the whole world—I mean, we're comparing it to **watches** and **Swiss Army Knives**—but it's got a cool name, so it's got that going for it.

Roche Towers
Giant, tooth-shaped buildings belonging to a pharmaceutical company that dominate the **Basel** skyline. **Expats** like working there because it means that they don't have to look at them from the outside.

Romands
The French-speaking Swiss. It's faster to say than "the French-speaking Swiss," so it's useful all around.

Romandy

French-speaking Switzerland. Divided from German-speaking Switzerland by the **Röstigraben**. Also referred to as Welschland, just to keep things confusing for newcomers.

Romansh

The language that you would think they speak in **Romandy** but instead is spoken in **Graubünden**. Romansh is one of the four official languages of Switzerland despite the fact that less than one percent of the population has it as a mother tongue. These people will generally also speak **German/Swiss German**.

There are several dialects of Romansh and they all are written differently. In fact, some dialects of Romansh are so different from each other as to be pretty much unintelligible. When Romansh speakers from these groups meet, they use Swiss German to communicate with each other.

You know your language is messed up when Swiss German is the better option.

Romansh Grischun

An artificial dialect of **Romansh** that was designed so that the speakers of the different dialects could all understand it. It is the official version and is used in official documents. I'm sure no one resents the fact that it was created by a *Zürcher*.

Rösti

The number one cause of grated potato kitchen disasters in Switzerland. The making of this dish requires flipping a panful of shredded potato in one go. Only the most advanced of experts own a perfectly sized plate for this task. Mere mortals are faced with the moral dilemma of whether to scoop half of the potato back into the pan or discard the possibly contaminated material. I know what I do.

Röstigraben

The geographic boundary dividing French-speaking Switzerland from German-speaking Switzerland.

The people on both sides generally learn the other language in school, but their fluency can vary to great degrees. Worse, the **Romands** learn **High German** and are subsequently confronted with **Swiss German** and can't understand a word. It is an extremely frustrating situation which often leads to both parties speaking **English** with each other to be understood.

The linguistic divide is also a cultural divide. And a political divide. There is often a marked difference with how the people on either side vote in a national referendum. The **Romands** tend to be more pro-**EU** than the German-speakers.

The truth, however, is in the name. The most important difference between these Swiss citizens is that the German-speaking ones like potatoes more.

RS – Rekrutenschule
This is where the **Swiss army** learns to army. Young men are sent off to RS to learn basic military procedures. They are thrown together with men from all across Switzerland. It's the ultimate male bonding experience. (See **mandatory military service**, **Swiss Army**.)

Rütlischwur
1291 is the date of the symbolic founding of Switzerland, the Rütlischwur. This was when the representatives from Uri, Schwyz and Unterwalden came together in the picturesque Rütli meadow above **Lake Luzern**, each stretching an arm into the air with two fingers and a thumb outstretched, swearing a secret pact of rebellion against the tyrannical ruling reeves of the time.

The Rütlischwur has come to represent the birth of Switzerland as a nation. The only problem is, no one knows if this vitally important event actually took place or not. Switzerland has collectively decided that this doesn't really matter. (See **Spiritual National Defence**.)

SAC hut

were separated. Children who were "illegally" born in Switzerland were forced to hide at home. But the railways got built, so that's cool.

Samichlaus
It is very important that you know that Samichlaus is not the same person as Santa Claus. They come on different days and are part of two different traditions. At the same time, if you ask how to say Santa Claus is in **Swiss German**, people will say Samichlaus. Before you get too worked up about the discrepancy, take a breath and realize that neither of them exist. (See also **Schmutzli**.)

Samichlaus day
The sixth of December is known as Samichlaus Day. Children are usually given chocolates, nuts, oranges and puffy bread-men known as *Grittibänz*.

SBB/CFF/FFS
A massive web of steel tracks holding the diverse regions of the country together. Without this binding transportation network, the country could fall apart into its constituent parts, the **Alps** spinning off to space and **Lugano** migrating to the mediterranean.

Schadenfreude
The joy of seeing your noisy neighbours get fined for putting their garbage out on the wrong day.

SAC hut
You sweat and pant, hiking for hours until you reach the end of the mountain valley. At this point you see a blue sign pointing to further up and a tiny building perched on an impossible slope. That is the SAC hut.

You thought you were hardcore, hiking six hours and sleeping overnight in the SAC hut? That's where you will meet twenty people even more outdoorsy than you, equipped with crampons and dehydrated food. Don't worry, you're still doing better than the Brits.

Sack of rice
Something that falls over in China whenever someone writes a boring article in German-speaking Europe.

Saisonnier
Foreign workers who were brought to Switzerland as labour, but subjected to inhumane restrictions on their immigration status. Families

Schaffhausen

The one canton in Switzerland where voting is mandatory and citizens who fail to cast their ballots have to pay a fine of a few francs. They take **direct democracy** seriously here. Possibly because they're surrounded on three sides by **Germany** and need to emphasize their **Swissness**.

Schellen-Ursli

The second-best-known Swiss children's book. Involves a boy named Ursli running away from his parents, hiking through hip deep snow and breaking into a mountain hut in order to be the boy carrying the biggest bell around. (See **Chaland-amarz**.) A good example of the male obsession with size.

In the film version, the story was expanded to include an avalanche, goat abduction and cheese fishing. Essential elements of any good story.

Schengen

Switzerland is a part of the Schengen Area, which allows free travel within its borders. This is particularly handy for the Swiss, who like to travel and buy things in countries where it's not as expensive as in Switzerland. (See **High Price Island**.)

Scherenschnitt

The art of paper cutting. Originally from China, but well-established in traditional Swiss handicraft. Here, it is mandatory to include at least one cow in every *Scherenschnitt* scene.

Schlager

"Music" that can only be appreciated while drunk. Famous German titles include "I want a cowboy for a husband" and "Breathless through the night". This is the soundtrack to many *Fasnacht* celebrations and **Après-Skis**.

Schmutzli

The bad cop to **Samichlaus**'s good cop. Schmutzli kidnaps misbehaving children, puts them in his sack and beats them with sticks. Or so the story goes. These days Schmutzli just shows up at a parade, waves his stick threateningly and disappears. Oh, and he has a donkey. That is somehow important.

Schneider-Ammann, Johann

Not actually a comedian, but rather a former Swiss president known for his expressionless speech about how laughter is good for your health. The smile-free clip was laughed at in countries all over the world. Mission accomplished, Johann.

Schnipo
Schnitzel with french fries *(Pommes)*. Typical **Après-Ski** food. What it lacks in nutritional value, it makes up for in grease.

Schnitzelbängg
Poetry slam for people who think poetry slam is too woke (Baslers). This *Fasnacht* tradition involves dressing up in masks and reciting rhyming verses that are humorous, clever and critical of society. In the costume, the performer is anonymous, so old, white men can use this as an opportunity to completely dispense with political correctness.

Schnitzeljagd
Disappointingly not a hunt for schnitzel.

Schoggiküss
A surprisingly racist chocolate-covered marshmallow.

Schönbächler, Richi
A kid who should have held on better, but didn't and became a part of Swiss television history.

The SRF documentary series *Auf und davon* follows Swiss families that emigrate to other countries. The Schönbächler family moved from Biel to the woods of Canada. In one scene, Richi's father tries to lower the four year old out of the cabin of an excavator machine. Richi falls and lets out a piteous yowl. Father Schönbächler responds with the immortal words: *"Richi, i ha dr doch gseit, söusch die guet häbe!!!"* "Richi, I told you to hold on tight!"

This phrase was instantly deemed to be uproariously funny and it is now considered appropriate to yell it at random opportunities.

And people say that the Swiss have no sense of humour …

Schrebergarten
Small allotment of land rented by people who don't have their own backyard. These can be used to grow food or flowers or for family gatherings. However, it is forbidden to permanently live on them. The waiting lists for them are prohibitively long, so only the most motivated get to have one. They should be called Strebergarten. Haha. That's a German joke that I made up. It's very funny, just trust me on this.

Schümli Pflümli
A sugary, alcoholic, coffee-based beverage. I highly recommend ordering one—not because it's particularly good, but because it's a lot of fun to say.

Schwägalp
A collection of consonants pretending to be a mountain.

Schwarzfahren
Riding public transportation without a valid ticket. Getting caught leads to a hefty fine and even worse, a whole tram full of people silently judging you.

Schwingen
A typically Swiss sport that looks very much like two grown men trying to give each other wedgies, but, as I've been assured, is nothing of the sort.

Schwingen is a type of wrestling in which participants wear diaper-like over-pants and face each other in a pit of sawdust. You grab your opponent firmly by the pants and he grabs you firmly by your pants and you try to force each other onto your backs. If you succeed, you win and you need to wipe the sawdust from his back in a collegial manner.

Women's Schwingen exists, but it's not yet as established as a serious sport. And yes, we're calling Schwingen a serious sport. Deal with it.

Schwingfest
A **Schwingen** competition. The largest of these events, *ESAF* "the Federal Schwingen and Alpine Festival", happens every three years. Alongside wrestling, it features traditional music and—crucially—approximately 250,000 litres of beer.

Schwingerkönig
The man who most successfully held on to other peoples pants without landing on his back in sawdust. According to tradition, the *Schwingerkönig* is not granted a monetary award, but instead, a cow. Generally referred to with the last name first and the first name last, just to be confusing.

Sechseläuten
A Zurich tradition involving an exploding wooden snowman (see **Böögg**), horses riding around in circles and bratwurst. The most important part is, of course, the bratwurst. These are grilled over the glowing remains of the Böögg. Kind of gruesome, when you think about it.

Secondo
This word refers to Swiss residents who are the children of immigrants. Born in Switzerland, but not necessarily Swiss citizens. You can tell that a population is well-represented in Switzerland when they have acquired their own particular ethnic slur. For

example "Tschingg" for Italians or "Jugo" for the diaspora from the parts of the former Yugoslavia. Canadians do not have their own insulting designation, despite my attempts to get *Ahornsirupschlürfer* ("Maple syrup slurper") into the Swiss vocabulary.

Self-control

Always carrying the appropriate ticket for public transportation.

Self-service cheese kiosks

As hiking routes often bring wanderers through farmer's fields dotted with **cow** patties, it seems only fair that these hikers are also given the opportunity to buy **cheese** and Swiss fudge (*Rahmtäfeli*) directly from the farmers.

This generally consists of a fridge and a money box inside an unattended shed and the whole affair operates on the honour system.

Foreigners are often impressed with the level of trust involved. What they may not realize is that the cost of paying a cashier Swiss wages would definitely cost more than any losses from theft. Furthermore, in the Swiss

Alps, one always has the feeling that one is being watched. (See **cows**).

Sempach, the battle of

An important battle in 1386 against the **Habsburgs** that helped solidify the early confederacy of Switzerland as a unit. Legend says the confederates won because of the heroic, self-sacrificing actions of one Arnold **Winkelried**. Or it could have been just too hot that day for the Habsburgs in their armour. The weather makes for a less interesting story, so let's stick to the Winkelried legend.

Serafe

"Swiss survey agency for the radio and television levy"

This is the newer version of **Billag**. Instead of going door to door and checking for radios and television, this agency just assumes that everyone has access to the internet and therefore access to Swiss television and radio and therefore has to pay the fee to support the public broadcaster.

However, this is not without advantages for the citizens. Those who pay the fee can now complain about any programming with the phrase: "I pay Billag for THIS????" (On these enlightened internet comment pages, the fee is often still referred to as Billag.) This phrase gives the citizen so much satisfaction, they comment it on any Swiss media, even those not supported by the fund.

Service public
Service provided by the state. This can include education, infrastructure, **SRF** and *Schadenfreude*.

Seven sinking steps
There is nothing more hilarious to the Swiss than one of their own politicians struggling to speak **English**, particularly if this politician is one of the richest people in Switzerland. The "seven sinking steps" is a phrase from an infamous 2015 video of Magdalena Martullo-Blocher giving a particularly unhelpful leadership seminar. The second most-quoted line is "You dreamer, du", a gift to Swiss meme-makers everywhere.

Sex Boxes
As you might have guessed from the name, these are boxes to have sex in. These drive-in sheds are slightly less glamorous than the name suggests.

Signposts
Switzerland has particularly good hiking signage. All over the country, convenient yellow signs tell wayward hikers which way the nearest town is, how long it takes to walk there and if there's food, a bus stop or a train station there. Those who follow the markings can't possibly go wrong. Until you do. (See **Rega**.)

Silvester
The German term for New Year's Eve.

Silvesterlauf
A foot race confusingly not occurring on New Year's Eve.

Sirenentest
On the first Wednesday of February sirens go off around the country. This is supposedly a test of the audio equipment. However, it has the side effect of trying the mental stability of newcomers, who hear the alarms and have to decide whether to panic or not.

Skiing
Sport characterized by paying exor-

WHOOOOoo...

bitantly to strap a slippery board to each foot and slide down a snow-covered mountain. In case you run into other people on the slope, you are equipped with a pokey stick in each hand.

Skilager
A place where small, innocent children are sent speeding down mountains.

Ski lifts

A place where skiers and snowboarders attempt to outmanoeuvre each other to the front of the pack for the honour of being the next to dangle many meters above the ground in the freezing cold air.

Ski touring

Involves hiking up a mountain with skis strapped to your back. Once you reach an appropriate height, you strap the boards to your feet and slide down the fresh snow unhindered by supervision or common sense.

Skijöring

A sport in which skiers are pulled along at speeds of up to 50 km/h behind horses, because normal skiing is far too safe.

Small talk

An opportunity to not only talk about the weather and current events, but to compare versions of **Swiss German**. If you are a foreigner you will undoubtedly be asked to say *Chuchichästli*, but among themselves the Swiss can also discuss dialects for hours. One must simply use a word that the others don't know (a common occurrence in mixed company) and it will give rise to a whole new round of discussion.

Snow

Either crystals of frozen water descending from the sky or cocaine. To determine which one is being referred to, check your immediate surroundings for scantily clad Germans and techno music. (See **Street Parade**.)

Snowboarding

Involves strapping both feet to one slippery, oblong board and sliding down a mountain covered in frozen crystals of water.

Snowli

A long-eared, white alien that helps small children learn how to ski.

Soccer (See *Fussball*.)

Sommerloch

"Summer Hole"
That time in the summer when the politicians are on vacation and there isn't much news to fill the papers.

This means that stories that at other times might not be judged newsworthy get the front page treatment. A sighting of a caiman in Hallwilersee, for one farfetched example, would be extensively covered.

Spanish Bread Railway
This was the first railway constructed entirely within Switzerland. It had nothing to do with Spain and nothing to do with bread. "Spanish Bread" was a pastry made in Baden and the railway allowed the specialty to be delivered fresh to the upper class folks in **Zurich**. This was basically all the railway was good for until it was connected to a larger network with more frequent service.

Spiritual National Defence
This was a cultural and political movement in the 1930s, a defence against the fascism on the rise in neighbouring countries. Swiss cultural heritage and democratic tradition was promoted as distinct from German and Italian culture. So this is probably where all of the cow stuff started. (See **advertising**.)

Spitzbuben
Literally "horny boys", these are of course jam filled cookies particularly popular around Christmas time. Too many horny boys are generally a bad thing.

Spyri, Johanna

Author of the children's book *Heidi*. Probably did more to promote Swiss tourism than anyone else in history, Roger Federer included. (See **Heidi**, **Heidbrunnen**, **Heididorf**, **Heidihof**, **Heidihaus**, **Heidihütte**, **Heidiland**, **Heidi Hotel** and **Heidiweg**.)

SRF/RTS/RSI

Switzerland's public broadcaster. Consists of diverse television, radio and online channels. SRF is charged with creating a sense of national identity; supporting Swiss musicians, artists and athletes; educating citizens who rely on this information in order to participate in Switzerland's direct democracy; and at the same time being entertaining. In four different languages. Easy, right? (See also **Serafe**, **Billag** and **insanity**.)

Standardized spelling

Something that doesn't exist in **Swiss German**. This can be a good or a bad thing, depending on how much you use your phone's autocorrect.

Ständemehr

A majority of the cantons. For popular initiatives and mandatory referendums, the majority of the people (*Volksmehr*) as well as a majority of cantons (*Ständemehr*) need to have voted yes. When the majority of the people vote yes, but not the majority of cantons, an initiative is said to have foundered on the Ständemehr. As "*mehr*" sounds like "*Meer*" (sea in German), this evokes images of paperwork sinking into the ocean. It's very poetic for politics.

St. Bernard

Breed of giant dog known for carrying a small barrel of brandy around its neck. The dog was bred for mountain rescue and the brandy was meant to revive the rescuee. Somehow this never caught on as an alcohol delivery method for **Après-Skis**. (See also **Barry**.)

St. Gallen

A city in eastern Switzerland best known for the fact that people there don't put mustard on their bratwurst.

St. Galler Bratwurst

The bratwurst that you're not supposed to put mustard on.

St. Galler Brot

A dense, moist bread, distinguished by the fact that it has a bump on the side that looks vaguely like a nose.

You're allowed to put mustard on it if you really, really want to.

St. Moritz

Ski town frequented by wealthy British tourists. St. Moritz hosted the 1928

Winter Olympics, where the Swiss tried to convince the world that **skijöring** was a good idea. (See also **White Turf**.)

Street Parade

A street party in **Zurich** characterized by techno music, provocative states of undress and drug use. A time-honoured Swiss tradition is to stay as far away from downtown Zurich on that day as possible.

Studentenschnitte

Chocolate cake made with stale cake or cookie crumbs. In this way, old cake is made into new cake. What no one is asking is why there was leftover cake or cookies to begin with.

Suckler Cows

The most dangerous version of **cows**: mothers. When a hiker is killed by a cow, it is almost always a mother cow protecting her suckling calves.

Suckler cows are not to be confused with "sucker" cows, which are cows that have been duped into taking part in multi-level-marketing schemes.

Summer

The season in which one spends hours walking up steep inclines despite the heat, the cows and common sense. (See **hiking**.)

Sunday

A day reserved for hiking in the mountains and the pursuit of non-commercial pastimes. Most stores are closed, funnelling desperate Sunday cookie bakers to the overcrowded, but thankfully open, train station grocery stores.

Super Bowl

An event that Swiss who have never been interested in American football will wake up at three a.m. to watch.

Mostly for the love of chicken wings, nachos and over-produced, yet witty commercials.

SVP
"*S'il vous plait*". This means "if you please" in French.

Swarovski Christmas tree
A tree decorated with Swarovski crystals that is erected in Zurich main train station during the Christmas season. It is huge. It is sparkly. And it doesn't do anything to disabuse visiting foreigners of the notion that Swiss people are all rich.

Swiss
When the Swiss talk about "Swiss", they are not talking about the Swiss and they are not talking about something that is Swiss. "Swiss" is what you find when you type swiss.ch in your computer's navigation bar. Swiss is German. It's a subsidiary of Lufthansa, a German airline.

Swiss Army, The
A sort of social club for Swiss men of a certain age. Here, a CEO and a truck driver can bond together over wet boots. It's like *Pfadi* (boy scouts) for adults.

Swiss Army Knife
The infamous multi-use pocket knife mostly used for opening wine bottles. Has ten functions you don't need and don't understand. But that one time you're in the woods and need to slice some *Landjäger*, you'll feel justified for bringing it along the other hundred times you didn't use it.

Swiss cheese
According to Americans, this is **cheese** with holes in it. It doesn't necessarily have to come from Switzerland. (See also **Emmentaler**, **AOP**.)

Swiss Cheese Union
A cartel formed during World War I in order to protect Swiss farmers from plummeting prices. It was disbanded in 1999 after several cheese-related corruption scandals.

Swiss citizenship
The most closely guarded of Swiss treasures. In most cases, it takes ten years official residence in order to be eligible for Swiss citizenship. And then you have an uphill battle in front of you, with tests of knowledge and language. And it costs a lot of money. And you could be disqualified because you once complained about **cowbells**.

Swiss flag

Some may say it's a big plus, but the most notable thing about the Swiss flag is that it's square. Switzerland is the only country in the whole world with a square flag. Except for the Vatican, which barely counts as country at all. If you really want to annoy the Swiss, draw it as a rectangle.

Swiss German

The name given to the collection of **German** dialects spoken in Switzerland. Swiss German is generally initially indecipherable to anyone who learned German elsewhere, including Germans. The Swiss will switch to **High German** to speak to you—if they have to—but they will probably resent you for it. Casually work the word *Chuchichästli* into the conversation a few times to appease them.

Swiss Guard

Colourfully dressed members of the **Swiss army** charged with guarding the Pope in the Vatican. The spiritual opposite of ninjas and the remnants of a Swiss mercenary tradition that saw Swiss soldiers fight in wars all over Europe.

Swiss humour

It exists. I swear.

Swiss Music Awards

An event where rectangular blocks of cement are given to musicians and they are happy about it.

Swiss Review

A free magazine sent to Swiss abroad to inform them about current events in Switzerland. The periodical is published in **English**, **German**, **French** and—of course—Spanish.

Swissair

The national airline of Switzerland that went bankrupt in 2002 and caused a national identity crisis. They don't like to talk about it.

Swissminiatur

A tourist attraction consisting of miniature versions of Swiss landmarks. A great place for people who have always wanted to feel like Godzilla.

Swissness

A marketing principle meaning to market a product using Swiss traditions and cultural icons. Swissness is often reduced to outdated clichés about traditional mountain life: **cows**, **cheese**, **chocolate**. Meanwhile, the vast majority of the population of Switzerland lives in urban areas.

By the way, "Swissness" is not a translation. They use the **English** word in **German**, **French** and **Italian**. Very Swiss of them.

Swissplaining

The act of explaining something not Swiss in Swiss terms.

Switzerland

Not Sweden.

Swissminiatur

Table bombs

Table bombs
Exploding cardboard tubes filled with items that are no longer interesting to small children after fifteen minutes.

Tap water
Swiss tap water is some of the best in the world, and free-flowing drinking fountains are found everywhere in cities. However, ordering tap water in restaurants still comes with a certain stigma. The Swiss would rather bite their tongues and order a bottle of environmentally unfriendly mineral water than risk people thinking they're being cheap. (See *Hahnenburger*, **Water**.)

Täschligate
Switzerland's greatest handbag-based scandal. Oprah Winfrey once visited Zurich and a shopkeeper refused to show her a crocodile-skin purse, because she assumed Oprah couldn't afford it. Oprah later told the story as an example of racism. This caused much debate in Switzerland and the whole affair was dubbed *"Täschligate"*. (*Täschli* is **Swiss German** for handbag.) The "-li" part denotes a diminutive, which makes the whole thing sound kind of cute.

Tatort
A beloved television series that rotates between following detective teams in different German, Austrian and Swiss cities. When a Swiss city has an episode, it is subject to extreme scrutiny by Swiss viewers and faces much tougher criticism than the other episodes.

The **Swiss German** spoken in these episodes is dubbed into **High German** for broadcast in **Germany** and **Austria**, so that they don't find out just how weird Swiss German actually is.

Teletext
A screen of primitive-looking, old-school computer text that appears on your television when you sit on your remote control in a particular way. Here you can inform yourself about the weather and current events. Many Swiss actually still use this as a way to keep updated, despite there being a newer, more attractive text-based information source known as the "internet".

Tell, William

A guy who refused to bow to a hat, shot an innocent apple, saved his jailers from a watery death and went on to gleefully assassinate the owner of the hat. Somehow manages to be the hero of Switzerland despite most likely being a Danish myth from 400 years earlier.

Thirteenth Salary

In Switzerland, it is common to divide your yearly salary into thirteen instalments, with the thirteenth being paid out together with the twelfth at the end of the year. This arrives just in time for you to blow it all buying overpriced trinkets and tiny dumplings at the **Christmas market**.

Ticino

The Italian-speaking canton of Switzerland. Overrun by German-speaking Swiss who want to go on vacation in a foreign land without actually leaving the country.

Thanks to its location south of the **Alps**, Ticino often enjoys a more Mediterranean climate than the rest of the country. This adds to its popularity as a vacation destination.

On holiday weekends, the **Gotthard** car tunnel that joins Ticino to the northern part of the country becomes the scene of a massive traffic jam, in which everyone is convinced that everyone else is the problem.

Ticket controllers

Most **public transportation** in Switzerland runs on the random check system. That means controllers come by every once in a while to check tickets and issue fines for those without them. Often a group of them will dress in plainclothes and enter every door of a tram at once, announcing their presence as soon as the doors close and the occupants are trapped. The realization that the exits are blocked and the ticket controllers are closing in always causes a spike of adrenaline, even if you have a valid ticket. Easy, Emily. It's going to be okay. (See also **Grüezi**.)

Tilt-Windows

Windows that open horizontally as well as tilting in vertically. This comes as a surprise to foreigners who think they've broken something when they first open one.

Time

Time runs differently in Switzerland. The first second of every minute lasts almost two normal seconds and the following 59 are slightly shorter to compensate. Don't believe me? Watch the official SBB clocks at any train station.

Tinguely, Jean

A Swiss artist known for his intricate moving sculptures and critique on consumerism. And this was in the sixties. Before Black Friday was a thing.

TipTopf

A cooking textbook for home economics classes that has been the best-selling Swiss schoolbook ever since its first edition in 1986. This popularity could be due to the useful tips and nutrition information, but I like to think that it's because of the clever word pun in the title (*Tipptopp* = excellent, *Topf* = pot).

Toast

Derogatory term for untoasted American-style, squishy sliced bread.

Toast Hawaii

A dish that has nothing to do with Hawaii. One can only love Toast Hawaii if one has been exposed to it from childhood. It, like Hawaiian pizza, suffers greatly from the inclusion of pineapple as an ingredient. The dish consists of a slice of **bread**, a slice of ham, a slice of **cheese**, a slice of pineapple and, breaking with the pattern, a whole cherry. Probably named by someone who was never in Hawaii.

Toblerone

A kind of **chocolate** that leaves things stuck in between your teeth. Its pyramidal shape has given rise to chocolate-centred conspiracy theories involving the Illuminati. However, the secret design hidden in the logo is simply a bear, the official animal of **Bern**.

Tourism

The only reason that the stores on **Bahnhofstrasse** are still in business.

Tourists

What Swiss people become when they visit other countries—a fact they conveniently forget while complaining about the tourists in **Luzern**.

Trail running

A pastime that consists of jogging on hiking terrain. A hobby for people who don't particularly care about preserving the cartilage in their joints, but love showing off their athleticism by passing out-of-breath hikers on the same trail.

Tram
A perfectly normal mode of transportation for furniture, moving boxes and giant inflatable **flamingos**.

Tram tracks
Bicycle wheel traps.

Turner, Tina
The best-selling Swiss artist of all time. Just because she wasn't a Swiss citizen at the time of being best-selling doesn't mean they don't get to claim her.

Trail running

Überfremdung

"Over-foreignisation"

This is the fear that foreign immigrants will take over Switzerland. This insecurity betrays a lack of faith in the country's ability to turn newcomers into mountain-loving, rule-abiding cheese-zealots. (See **Pick-me expat**.)

Urban-rural divide

A social and political division that is possibly more important than the **Röstigraben**, the **Polentagraben** and the **Brünig-Napf-Reuss Line** combined. It is, however, less important than the applesauce-on-or-next-to-the-*Älplermagronen* conflict, if you happen to be eating *Älplermagronen* at the time.

User fees

One of the interesting and creative ways that Switzerland sucks money out of you in order to keep its taxes low. (See also **fee bags**.)

Vita parcours

Valais

A bilingual canton of Switzerland known for its wine, rugged mountains and indecipherable **Valais German**.

Valais German

The type of **Swiss German** spoken in the mountain region of **Valais**. Known to be almost completely incomprehensible to the rest of the country. The Valais people are as proud of this as all Swiss German speakers are proud that people from **Germany** can't understand Swiss German. (See also **Puttitschiffra**.)

Vermicelles

Beloved Swiss dessert made out of chestnuts that rather disturbingly resembles a pile of worms.

Vignette

A sticker that you need buy to be allowed to drive on the highways every year. Sticker fees help pay for all of the construction slowing down your commute home. The stickers are designed to be so difficult to remove that you have to buy a special tool to scrape it off of your windshield—a fact that is very convenient for manufacturers of Vignette-Scraper-Off-ers.

Vita parcours

Simple outdoor exercise courses consisting mostly of logs to jump over, logs to stand on and bars to dangle from. Thankfully located in wooded areas so there are fewer witnesses to my lack of coordination.

Volksfest (See **Wümmetfest**.)

Volksnah

"Close to the people."
Politicians demonstrate their approachability by doing photo-ops with livestock (see **OLMA**) and taking public transportation.

is British slang for masturbation and accept the fact that tourists smirk when they see the Wankdorf train station sign. And if they don't, well, now they know. Please never change.

Waschküche
"Wash-kitchen"
The battlefield of the apartment building. (See **Waschplan**.)

Waschplan
A system that brings order to the chaos of the communal laundry room of an apartment building. It is the primary cause of passive-aggressive post-it wars between neighbours. The *Waschplan* manifests itself most often as a calendar hung in the laundry room with washing time slots that residents can sign up for—even up to a year in advance. Some buildings may have no written schedule, but this does not mean that there is no plan. An unwritten *Waschplan* may have slowly coalesced in the minds of the longtime residents and must be taken as seriously as any codified law.

Written or unwritten, this laundry schedule must be strictly adhered to, for fear of attracting the wrath of the most terrifying creature in all of Switzerland. (See **Bünzli**.)

Waffenlauf
"Weapon-Run"
The treasured Swiss tradition of going for a jog while carrying your rifle.

Wandergruppe
Gangs of retirees that roam the **Alps**, arriving at the Beiz just moments before you, taking up the best places on the patio.

Wankdorf
The place where the **Young Boys** play. This is a real neighbourhood that exists. At this point, the Swiss have probably realized that "wank"

Watches
Making wrists more judgmental since 1542.

Water

Precious national resource that the Swiss are convinced is worth 400x more when infused with carbon dioxide and packaged in plastic.

Weggli

Butt-shaped bread, commonly eaten with a brown chocolate log.

Wellness

Spas, saunas and that sort of thing. Basically an excuse to be naked and traumatize prudish foreigners.

Welsch

In Switzerland, this is does not mean the residents of Wales, but of **Romandy**.

Welschland (See **Romandy**.)

Wetterfrosch
"Weather Frog"

This is not an actual frog, but in fact a human being who tells us what the weather will be like in the future, often from the roof of a building in Oerlikon.

Wetterschmöcker

Literally "Weather smeller", these are slightly unconventional weather prophets. They are more likely to talk to ants than your average Swiss.

White Turf

A horse-racing competition that takes place in February on the frozen lake of **St. Moritz**. The winner gets named the "King" of **Engadin**.

The horses wear special shoes that grip the snow better. The spectators wear expensive furs and sip champagne before going back to their 1000 CHF per night hotel rooms.

Will of the people

Something is considered to be the will of the people when 18% of the population of Switzerland vote for it.

Willensnation

Switzerland is considered to be a nation of the will, because of all the people of disparate language and religious backgrounds that are joined together in one country. The only thing keeping them together is their "will". And possibly money and a shared disdain for the neighbouring countries.

Winkelried

The hero of the **Battle of Sempach**. According to the legend, he died by throwing himself on the Habsburger pikes, allowing the confederates to break through the line. Like many Swiss heroes, he probably didn't really exist.

Winter
Something terrible that needs to be scared off at all costs. (See *Chalandamarz*, **Böögg**, *Guggenmusik* and **Schlager**.)

Winzerfest (See **Quartierfest**.)

WK
"Refresher course"
After **RS**, unless the recruit has opted to do his military service in one long stretch, he has to come back for a refresher course. It's like coming back to summer camp to see all your old friends again. But with more assault rifles.

Women's Suffrage
Because of Switzerland's system of **direct democracy**, in order for women to acquire the right to vote, a majority of the voting population (men) needed to vote for it. Several initiatives for women's suffrage were rejected, most recently in 1959, when two thirds of voters were still against it. However in 1971, the numbers had flipped and two thirds voted to finally allow women to vote.

On the cantonal level, Appenzell Innerrhoden refused to give women the vote until 1990, when the supreme court forced them to.

Despite the fears of the "No"-campaigners, the subsequent generations of Swiss children with voting mothers grew up just fine. It turns out, women can multitask.

Work-life-balance
According to the Valais tourist board, in **Valais** it's a life-work-balance. Very clever. Let's all move there.

World Economic Forum (WEF)
An international, non-governmental organization that has its annual meeting in Davos, Switzerland. Here, the world's richest and most powerful people get to have their view ruined by a giant **golden egg**.

Wümmetfest (See *Winzerfest*.)

YB

Young Boys. A soccer team based in **Bern**. Kind of an infantilizing name, if you ask me, but no one asked me. (See **Wankdorf**.)

Yellow diamonds

The landscape of Switzerland is dotted with yellow diamonds. By this, I do not mean precious gems, but rather small metal or painted diamond-shaped signs. These marks keep errant wanderers on the official hiking paths. (See **signposts**.)

Yodelling

A treasured vocal tradition. That this comes from the same country that produced the guttural sounds of **Swiss German** is a tribute to the elasticity of the human vocal system.

Zombies

Zibelemärit

This "onion market" is a festival that takes place on the fourth Monday of November in **Bern**. This is very convenient for the people who only buy onions once a year and like getting **confetti** thrown at them while they do it.

Zimmerstunde

Split opening hours. This is the reason the only restaurant in town is closed when your hike was too long and you get back to town at three in the afternoon. Not that I'm still bitter about it, Restaurant Sternen.

Znüni

The Swiss know about second breakfast, traditionally eaten around nine o'clock in the morning. This almost makes up for the fact that they think you can start brunch at one o'clock.

Zooglers

Google employees who work in the **Zurich** office. Get it? Because Z for Zurich and "oogle" for Google. So clever!

Zombies

Not likely to be a problem in Switzerland. Firstly, because of the abundant amount of guns distributed throughout the country thanks to Switzerland's compulsory military service and secondly, because they don't exist.

Zopf

Braided bread. Leftover Zopf makes great French Toast/*Fotzelschnitte*. Or it would, if there was ever any leftover *Zopf*.

Zug

The **canton** with the lowest income tax. Or the train you take to get there. Don't get them confused. We wouldn't want you to try living in a train. I'm sure the taxman would find you there anyway.

Zurich

One big construction site often mistakenly referred to as the capital of Switzerland. (See also **Baur au Lac**.)

Zwingli, Huldrych

The Swiss Martin Luther. He was an important leader of the Reformation movement in **Zurich** and fell in battle against the Catholics in 1531. When his enemies found him among the wounded, they killed him. And then

they quartered his body, burned it
and mixed the ashes with dung.

Zytglogge

The famous clock tower in **Bern**. I
don't have a joke here, I just didn't
want to end the book on **Zwingli**.
Depressing shit.

AUTHOR BIO

Emily Engkent was born on the date of her birth in a hospital in Canada. At the ripe old age of 27, she came to live in Switzerland where her accomplishments include learning Swiss German, teaching the locals about orange cheese and impersonating a hamster. She is mildly Internet-famous because of *Emily National*, her video series on watson.ch about being a foreigner in Switzerland. She could be considered the most famous Canadian in Switzerland, but unfortunately her arch-nemesis Shania Twain also lives here. Damn you, Shania.

BIBLIOGRAPHY

Andrey, Georges. *Schweizer Geschichte für Dummies*. WILEY-VCH Verlag GmbH & Co. KGaA, Weinheim, 2007.

Bewes, Diccon. *Swiss Watching: Inside Europe's Landlocked Island*. Nicholas Brealey Publishing. London, 2010.

Bilton, Paul. *Xenophobe's Guide to the Swiss*. Xenophobe's Guides. London. 2013.

Jans, Beat, Guy Krneta & Matthias Zehnder (Hrsg.) *Unsere Schweiz: Ein Heimatbuch für Weltoffene*. Zytglogge Verlag AG, Basel, 2019.

Küng, Thomas. *Gebrauchsanweisung für die Schweiz*. Piper Verlag GmbH, Munich, 2002.

Mettan, Guy & Christophe Büchi. *(Tout) Nouveau Dictionnaire Impertinent de la Suisse*. Slatkine. Geneva, 2019.

New, Mitya. *Switzerland Unwrapped: Exposing the Myths*. I.B. Publishers. London, 1997.

O'Dea, Claire. *The Naked Swiss*. Bergli Books. Basel, 2018.

Oertig-Davidson, Margaret. *Beyond Chocolate: Understanding Swiss Culture*. Bergli Books. Basel, 2002.

Richter, Bettina & Jakob Tanner. *Ja! Nein! Yes! No! Swiss Posters for Democracy*. Lars Müller Publishers. Zurich, 2021.

Steinberg, Jonathan. *Why Switzerland?* University Printing House, Cambridge. 2015

Willmeroth, Sandra & Fredy Hämmerli. *Exgüsi: Ein Knigge für Deutsche und Schweizer zur Vermeidung grober Missverständnisse*. Orell Füssli Verlag AG. Zurich, 2009.

Wurzenberger, Gerda & Nicole Schiferer (HRSG). *Die Schweiz in der Vernehmlassung*. Kein und Aber AG. Zürich, 2003.

Zollinger, Marc. *Globi und die Demokratie*, Globi Verlag. Zurich, 2018.

Gotthard Tunnel

ACKNOWLEDGMENTS

This book would not have been possible without the patience of all of the Swiss people who have interacted with me throughout the years. And even more so, the Swiss friends (I swear I have some) who I have forced to read drafts of this book: Dani Huber, Sonja Bugmann, Fabio Vonarburg, Andie Pilot, Samuel Bucheli, Lea Senn, Michelle Marti and Sarah Serafini. Thank you for catching my mistakes and mitigating my self-doubt.

I also consulted with regional experts. And by that, I mean, friends that happen to be from particular parts of the country. For my entries on **Valais**, I double-checked with Sergio Minnig. For **Basel**, Martina Stadelmann. For **Romandy**, Saïnath Bovay. Though to be completely fair, I just handed Saïnath a list of Romandy-related terms at the watson Christmas party, at a point in the evening when we were all decently sloshed. It's quite possible he missed something, squinting at the print-out in the disco lighting.

I would like to thank my parents, who are authors themselves, for their help. My mother for went through the whole book with me, telling me what she didn't understand and dealing with my snark. My sister had to put up with me texting her random questions like: "Do you think the phrase 'Suck it, Zurich' is too vulgar?" and "Do you recognize this guitar riff? Dun, dun, DUUUN, dun, dun, DA-DUUUN, dun, dun, DUUNN, DUH-dunnnnnnn." She didn't, but I put it in the book anyway.

My editor at Bergli Books, Richard Harvell, was a great help and painstakingly went through the different drafts I sent him at irregular intervals. His many inputs were vital, despite him mistakenly thinking that a *caquelon* would be too small to wear as a hat. I tried one on at work to be sure, and it was rather on the too big side. Which means one could theoretically wear it as a hat with the appropriate padding.

The translator for the German version of this book, Lucas Schmidli, is also a friend of mine and was also plagued with multiple versions and demands for feedback. Thank you for your fortitude.

I would NOT like to thank Maurice Thiriet, my boss at watson, who, every time I mentioned this project, would talk about how another coworker took time off to write a book and never finished it. Mo, that was very discouraging.

www.ingramcontent.com/pod-product-compliance
Lightning Source LLC
Chambersburg PA
CBHW041345150426
42813CB00057BA/2712